WORLD WAR 1:

A Complete History of WW1 and Its Modern Impact

History Brought Alive

© Copyright 2025 - All rights reserved.

Published 2025 by History Brought Alive

The content contained within this book may not be reproduced, duplicated, or transmitted without direct written permission from the author or the publisher.

Under no circumstances will any blame or legal responsibility be held against the publisher, or author, for any damages, reparation, or monetary loss due to the information contained within this book, either directly or indirectly.

LEGAL NOTICE

This book is copyright protected. It is only for personal use. You cannot amend, distribute, sell, use, quote, or paraphrase any part, or the content within this book, without the consent of the author or publisher.

DISCLAIMER NOTICE

Please note the information contained within this document is for educational and entertainment purposes only. All effort has been made to present accurate, up-to-date, reliable, complete information. No warranties of any kind are declared or implied. Readers acknowledge that the author is not engaged in the rendering of legal, financial, medical, or professional advice. The content within this book has been derived from various sources. Please consult a licensed professional before attempting any techniques outlined in this book.

By reading this document, the reader agrees that under no circumstances is the author responsible for any losses, direct or indirect, that are incurred as a result of the use of the information contained within this document, including, but not limited to, errors, omissions, or inaccuracies.

FREE BONUS FROM HBA: EBOOK BUNDLE

Greetings!

First, thank you for reading our books.

Now, we invite you to join our VIP list. As a welcome gift we offer the History & Mythology eBook Bundle below for free. Plus, you can be the first to receive new books and exclusives! <u>Remember it's 100% free to join.</u>

Simply click the link below to join.

https://www.subscribepage.com/hba

Keep up to date with us on:
YouTube: History Brought Alive
Facebook: History Brought Alive
www.historybroughtalive.com

TABLE OF CONTENTS

Introduction 1

Chapter 1: The Road to War 5

Chapter 2: The War to End All Wars 17

Chapter 3: The Human Cost of War....................................... 35

Chapter 4: Innovation, Destruction, and Healing..................... 59

Chapter 5: The Spread of War 79

Chapter 6: Lessons for Today... 101

Chapter 7: The Horrors of Trench Warfare 119

Chapter 8: The Last Thunderclap 131

Chapter 9: How People Rebuilt After the War......................... 141

Chapter 10: Freedom's Bitter Taste 153

Conclusion 169

References:... 173

Introduction

World War I, also known as the *Great War*, was a major 20th-century global conflict, one that changed the world forever. It redrew maps, toppled empires, and introduced a new and revolutionary kind of warfare that would shape the conflicts of the entire era and beyond. As it was such a significant period in our shared history, as well as a conflict that affected the entire globe, it is always a challenging topic to write about. The sheer magnitude of the first true *world war* is the initial obstacle writers tackle even before a single word is written. How can we truly reflect on the millions of lives lost in the whirlwind of that devastating war? How can we effectively consider all the war-torn corners of the world and deliver the stories of all those who suffered? After all, beyond the trenches and the treaties, beyond the strategies and the thundering guns, this was a war fought by *people*. Young men and women, soldiers leaving their homes in their blooming youth, nurses risking their lives to save the wounded, and politicians above them all making life and death decisions. Their shared stories, filled with fear, sacrifice, love, and courage, are what truly bring World War I to life.

So, in order to deliver the vision of the First World War that needs to be seen and properly understood, we need to approach it from a different perspective and view it through the lens of compassion, understanding, and common sense. Because, after all, the human sacrifice needs to be addressed, from the trenches of the Western Front all the way to the sweeping hand-to-hand battles in the Balkans, and even to the illustrious air battles of the flying pioneers. Of course, many of the modern Great War books usually focus on the grander aspects of this war: the great strategies, the complex politics, and the intricate battle tactics. These are, certainly, quite important topics, but they often leave out the very thing that makes history matter: the human experience. It is time to change that. So, rather than just recounting statistics, names, and dates and rendering the human element unimportant, we will attempt to step into the shoes of the people who lived through this terrible war.

The First World War is often viewed as a distant, black-and-white event, a war that is well beyond our own era and disconnected from our lives. But this is far from the truth. The Great War's echoes still resound in the world today. Of course, much has changed since those blood-soaked first decades of the 20th century. Additionally, the world was even more restless in the years that followed and was never truly the same. But no conflict that came after could match the sheer scale and brutality of that great old macabre giant that today we call the First World War. For this was truly the era in which the oppressed nations of the world cried in unison for their freedoms, and the world held its breath in anticipation.

From those early months of 1914, as the entire globe waited fearfully and impatiently, proud and venerable Europe stood on the precipice, over the abyss that was war.

Sadly, the ferocious tides of war could not be avoided. Europe plunged headfirst into war, and the rest of the world followed closely behind. What started as a conflict between two nations escalated into the first true global conflict that was the Great War. It lasted from the 28th of July, 1914, to the 11th of November, 1918, and claimed millions upon millions of lives. Today, the First World War is regarded as one of the deadliest conflicts in human history, and one that came at a tremendous cost for Europe: 60 million of the continent's sons and daughters perished in the flames of war.

WORLD WAR 1

Throughout this book, we will journey through the battlefields of the Western Front, the shifting alliances of global politics, and the home fronts where everyday people struggled to survive. But more importantly, we will meet individuals whose names never made it into the history textbooks but whose experiences profoundly shaped the world. The goal is not just to inform but to immerse, not just to educate but to engage.

This is the story of World War I as it was lived, felt, and remembered. A war that, though fought over a century ago, still speaks to us today. Let us step back into history, not just to understand the past, but to illuminate the present and the future.

Chapter 1: The Road to War

At the dawn of the Great War, many crucial events occurred that set the stage for conflict. But even before that, the world experienced a series of key changes and developments with the onset of the 20th century. Often unequal and dynamic, they were paramount in shaping the world in a way that led to global war. And of all the changes that occurred, the most important involved *industry*. In a very short period, the world transformed from old traditions and archaic ways to major industries and modern technologies. At first, large-scale industries were reserved for the major urban centers of Europe. All the while, the rural areas continued in their traditional lifestyles. But this would change quickly, as the world's focus shifted toward rapid industrialization. And nothing would be the same again,

With the rise of industrialization in Europe, urbanization became the norm. Major metropolitan centers emerged, triggering significant demographic shifts across the continent — changes that would later shape the scale and structure of World War I. The gradual appearance of large corporations and factories, all of which employed thousands of workers, and the shift from steam engines to ones powered by petrol and diesel, made it clear that Europe — and the rest of the world — was heading into a brand-new age, an age in which the traditional rural ways of life were rapidly fading out.

The resulting demographic changes were instrumental in shaping the story of how the Great War emerged. At the beginning of the century, the European continent experienced a true population "boom." Large migrations became the norm, spurred by the call from large industries for a workforce, and soon many Europeans journeyed far across the world, seeking new opportunities in North America, where work was plentiful. Those who remained in Europe discovered new opportunities in a rapidly changing world. People began moving into urban centers and emerging communities, and many cities experienced dramatic growth in no more than a decade.

Such rapid change was the most significant contributor to major class differences: industrial growth and increased commerce were a new source of wealth, from which arose a professional, commercial, white collar middle class. On the other hand, the increase in population and the move

WORLD WAR 1

from rural communities into the rapidly growing cities resulted in substantial poverty levels for the lower-class, blue-collar working families, who often had around four children each on average and had to live in underdeveloped apartment blocks in usually squalid conditions. The significant gap between the classes gradually became quite apparent in every aspect of early 20th-century life. Segregation in urban environments increased, with a huge difference in dress and social habits between the rich and poor.

The leading global power that emerged from the Industrial Revolution of the mid-19th century was Great Britain. It rapidly rose to become a looming, global industrial giant and was often referred to as the "world's workshop" as a result. But Britain was not alone in its race to power. Other major European powers soon caught up, creating a large rush toward power and modernization. Germany ran neck-and-neck with Britain, and by the 1870s, it rapidly expanded its industries, emerging as the top producer of coal, iron, and steel. By 1913, it had replaced Britain as the world's leader. Of course, there was always a bigger "giant." The largest industrial power on the planet was not in Europe, but rather lay across the ocean: the United States. It stood as an enormous, well-oiled machine, uncontested in its leadership of the newly emerging industrial world. But all this contributed to the appearance of a significant power imbalance. In Europe, small nations struggled to compete with the major powers. They could not match Germany's growth, resulting in major shifts in power levels between nations. And such an imbalance could not be fixed; it would result in profound implications later.

But beyond the changing global hierarchy, an even greater threat to balance emerged: *nationalism*. By the early 20th century, nationalism arose as the defining political force all across Europe. It bound people together, but all the while it sowed division and hate. While nationalism fostered unity within established nation-states, it also fueled separatist movements and inter-state rivalries. To make matters worse, rapid industrialization had given all nations the means to mass-produce weapons of war. And with many inter-ethnic tensions weaving a tangled web of alliances, this meant that any conflict, even a small one, could quickly spiral out of control. As a result, nationalism became a key force in unraveling the stability of Europe's political landscape. Nowhere was this more apparent than in the Balkans, where ethnic and political tensions continually threatened regional stability.

WORLD WAR 1

Known as the "powder keg of Europe," the Balkan Peninsula was home to numerous nationalist movements seeking independence from the weakening Ottoman Empire. With Russian backing, Serbia aimed to create an independent state for all South Slavs, bringing it into direct conflict with Austria-Hungary, which sought to suppress Slavic nationalism within its own borders. As a multi-ethnic empire, Austria-Hungary faced internal nationalist agitation from the Czechs, Slovaks, Serbs, Croats, and other ethnic groups living within the empire. The empire's inability to effectively address their demands for autonomy contributed to internal instability and external conflicts, particularly regarding Serbia.

Then there was German nationalism, fueled by its economic and military strength, which contributed to a sense of superiority and competition, particularly with neighboring France. France, still resentful over the loss of Alsace-Lorraine in the Franco-Prussian War (1870 to 1871), pursued policies aimed at containing Germany.

Russia also loomed close by and positioned itself as the protector of the Slavic peoples, particularly in the Balkans. That put it at odds with Austria-Hungary and contributed to Russian support for Serbia, which became a significant factor in the

WORLD WAR 1

outbreak of World War I.

As such, throughout much of the 19th century, Europe's leading powers grappled with maintaining a fragile peace. Their struggles led to the creation of numerous complex military alliances and trade deals. Following the German unification, the aged German chancellor, Otto Von Bismarck—the head of Europe's dominant nation—employed a strategy that, generally, sought to maintain peace by preserving a balance of power and preventing a two-front war. He did so by holding all the competing states in check. He arbitrated the dealings between Russia and Austria-Hungary and kept France in diplomatic isolation and without any significant allies. He was the creator of several highly important and ingenious treaties and alliances, which benefited both Europe and Germany. One of these was the Reinsurance Treaty, effective from 1897 to 1890, a diplomatic agreement between Russia and Germany that ensured their neutrality in the event either nation entered a war with a major power. Sadly, this treaty was one of the last assurances of peace in Europe; as soon as Bismarck resigned from his position in 1890, his policies and his efforts were soon to be undone. His departure led to a shift in German foreign policy, resulting in the deterioration of

German-Russian relations and the subsequent Franco-Russian Alliance (1894), which laid the foundation for the eventual Triple Entente.

Archduke Franz Ferdinand minutes before his assassination, 1914.

The Reinsurance Treaty, that fragile hold on peace, was quickly forgotten. It lapsed and was replaced by the Dual Alliance, a new defensive treaty between Germany and Austria-Hungary. Over time, they expanded their alliance by bringing Italy into the fold. This was all the work of Bismarck's unskilled successor, the new Chancellor Leo von Caprivi, who greatly lacked his predecessor's diplomatic and nation-leading abilities. His missteps ultimately contributed to the emergence of two opposing alliance blocks, and each ally felt obliged to aid the other in the event of war. In the late 19th and early 20th centuries, the rivalry between Germany and Great Britain intensified as well, expanding in scale and significance. As competition for dominance in Europe grew, tensions between the two nations increased, leading to an arms race, which quickly centered on naval power.

In 1897, German Admiral Alfred von Tirpitz initiated the Anglo-German Naval Race with a plan to build a formidable fleet that could challenge Britain and pressure it into making diplomatic concessions. However, in reality, this German fleet would function primarily as a "fleet in being" — intended to exert influence while remaining in port rather than securing outright victory in a naval conflict. Tirpitz, serving as naval secretary under Kaiser Wilhelm II, firmly believed that naval supremacy was key to gaining political leverage over Britain. Enthusiastic about German expansion and maritime power, the Kaiser endorsed Tirpitz's vision and set his plan into motion.

The German Reich Navy Office embarked on an ambitious, long-term fleet expansion, aiming to build no fewer than 60 large battleships. The evolving nature of naval warfare required a shift in strategy. Speed and raiding tactics gave way to a focus on sheer tonnage, size, and heavily armed warships capable of enduring sustained enemy fire.

However, Germany's aggressive naval expansion placed a heavy burden on its economy and infrastructure. In 1908, the Reichstag passed a fourth naval bill, accelerating production to four battleships per year. That same year, however, the outbreak of the Bosnian Crisis forced Germany to divert a significant portion of its budget toward its army. Chancellor Bernhard von Bülow ultimately recognized that Germany could not sustain both the largest land force in Europe and a dominant navy, casting doubt on Tirpitz's grand vision.

All this pointed to the fact that, as empires expanded, fueled by their new industries and wealth, they were at the same time marred by deep tensions, unresolved territorial disputes, and simmering hostilities. And it was against this dark backdrop, when the planet teetered on the edge of the abyss, that one key event would tip the world into unbounded catastrophe. And that event was the assassination of Archduke Franz Ferdinand of Austria-Hungary on June 28th, 1914.

On that fateful summer day, the heir to the Austro-Hungarian throne and his wife, Sophie, traveled to Sarajevo. The city, part of the empire but inhabited by many Serbs and other South Slavic ethnicities who resented foreign rule, was a hotbed of nationalist sentiment. A small but determined group of Serbian nationalists, known as the Black Hand (*Црна Рука*), had plotted the Archduke's assassination. They believed that by killing the Archduke, they could spark a revolution that would lead to independence for all Slavic nationalities under Austria-Hungary.

The first assassination attempt failed. A grenade thrown at the royal motorcade by a member of the Black Hand missed its target and injured several spectators and members of the Archduke's entourage. The Archduke was unharmed, and the convoy continued on its way. It appeared that he had escaped death, but fate had other plans. Later that day, as Archduke Ferdinand's driver took a wrong turn, the car came to an unexpected stop directly in front of Gavrilo Princip, a 19-year-old Serb nationalist who was armed with a pistol. Seizing the moment, the young man fired two shots. Within moments, the Archduke and his wife lay dying. *This* was the event that plunged the world into chaos. A decisive freedom fighter seeking independence for his oppressed compatriots acted on his passions and shot the leader of his enemies dead. Like a stone plunged into a pond, its impact sent ripples throughout Europe. News of the assassination spread rapidly, and Europe was shocked. What should have been a localized act of violence instead triggered a major chain reaction. Austria-Hungary, eager to assert its dominance, blamed Serbia for the killing and declared war on July 28th, 1914. Russia, bound by its alliance with Serbia, mobilized its forces in response. Germany, allied with Austria-Hungary, saw Russian mobilization as a direct threat and declared war on Russia. France, aligned with Russia, was soon drawn in. It was a cascade of declarations of war. When Germany invaded neutral Belgium to reach France, Britain had no choice but to declare war on Germany. Within weeks, what had started as a regional crisis had spiraled into a global conflict.

Chapter 2:
The War to End All Wars

The all-too-rapid path toward a full-scale European conflict was swift and decisive. Following Archduke Ferdinand's assassination in Sarajevo, the Serbian government knew that Austria-Hungary's wrath was inevitable. They also knew that the terms and demands in the Austro-Hungarian ultimatum would be far from acceptable. So, expecting the worst, the Serbs prepared by ordering complete mobilization the very next day.

Austria-Hungary followed suit, with Emperor Franz Joseph ordering the mobilization of a full eight army corps, which were to begin combat operations against Serbia. The public in Vienna was delighted by the declaration of war. Meanwhile, in order to create a more decisive political stance, and to offer some semblance of support toward Serbia, Russia ordered a partial mobilization against Austria-Hungary. Russia's primary intent was to deter Austria-Hungary from actually carrying out the attack on the small Balkan nation. This was followed by further orders from Tsar Nicholas II, with which he decided to step into the conflict between Serbia and Austria-Hungary by putting his armies on general alert. Following these significant steps from Russia, German Kaiser Wilhelm II asked the Tsar (who was his cousin) to cancel the call for mobilization and step back. When the Tsar refused, Germany declared war on Russia. Germany also sent an ultimatum to France demanding her neutrality under which France was not to aid Russia if it got involved in Serbia's defense.

The French ignored the ultimatum altogether, which Germany had expected. Nonetheless, France desired to avoid the conflict. The French urged restraint, with French Premier Rene Viviani sending a direct message to St. Petersburg, asking that Russia abstain from any actions that would provoke war with Germany.

Furthermore, as a sign of their peaceful intentions, the French army ordered all troops to retreat some 10 kilometers (6.2 miles) inland and away from the German border. Even so, with both the British and the French advocating against a widespread conflict, Germany and Austria-Hungary steadily continued their move toward conflict. Russia continued its mobilization, with faint assurances that it was not intended as a prelude to war. And when the Russian partial mobilization turned into a general one, Germany reacted. Kaiser Wilhelm signed the order for the general mobilization of the German Army, which immediately began its operations to invade Belgium and Luxembourg — a part of their plan to invade France.

The die was cast.

War on France was officially declared by Germany on August 3rd, and on Russia two days before that, …" with "Germany officially declared war on Russia on August 1st and, two days later, on France on August 3rd. This drew in Great Britain. The British ambassador to Germany, Sir Edward Goschen, delivered an ultimatum to the German Ministry of Foreign Affairs, demanding an immediate end to the violation of Belgian neutrality. When Germany did not accept the ultimatum, Great Britain declared war on Germany on August 4th, 1914.

Lastly, Austria-Hungary declared war on Russia on August 6th. Within just a few days, all of Europe's major powers were at war with one another, initiating a conflict of enormous scale. The widespread calls for mobilization and volunteer enlistment across Europe meant the conscription of millions of men.

Bloodshed loomed on the horizon.

German soldiers on the way to the Front, 1914.

The first operations of the war occurred in Serbia. At the start of hostilities, the small Slavic nation was able to field noticeably fewer men than Austria-Hungary. Furthermore, the Austro-Hungarians were much better equipped in every way. In 1914, General Oskar Potiorek was responsible for Austria-Hungary's southern (Serbian) front. He commanded approximately 500,000 men in 329 battalions. In comparison, the defending Serbian Army and its ally, Montenegro, had some 344,000 troops in 209 battalions. Despite this disparity, the opening stages of the Austro-Hungarian campaign against Serbia would surprise everyone.

The so-called "Serbian Campaign" began almost immediately after Austria-Hungary declared war on July 28th, 1914, when they shelled the Serbian capital, Belgrade, the very next day. A flotilla of river patrol boats sailed up the river Danube under the cover of darkness and stopped across the river from the capital. At 1:00 am, they commenced a heavy bombardment of the city. One of these boats, the SMS Bodrog, was credited with firing the first shots of the Great War.

Almost three weeks later, the eager General Potiorek started his offensive against Serbia. He was motivated by a desire to knock Serbia out of the war as swiftly as possible, ideally before the emperor's birthday. Certain of his success, he ordered his entire Fifth Army, and only a small portion of his Second Army, to enter Serbia from northern Bosnia. The experienced Serbian commanders were surprised by the unexpected direction of the attack, but managed to promptly direct their forces to meet the invaders. Led by the seasoned Marshal Radomir Putnik, the Serbian army faced the Austro-Hungarians on the Cer

WORLD WAR 1

Mountain in hilly western Serbia. During a harsh four-day battle, lasting from August 15th to 24th, the Serbians greeted the Austro-Hungarians with a proper surprise.

The first clash in this decisive battle occurred during the dark of night (and almost by accident) when the forward elements of the 1st Combined Division of the Serbian army encountered Austro-Hungarian outposts. What started out as some light skirmishing soon erupted into a pitched battle over a wide front.

Combat experience quickly became a defining factor in the battle's flow. The largely inexperienced Austro-Hungarian soldiers were quick to flee from determined and fierce attacks by battle-hardened Serbian soldiers. Major clashes occurred in the retaking of the surrounding towns of Kosanin Grad and Šabac. The Serbs subjected Kosanin Grad to repeated assaults, but were continually repulsed by the dug-in Austro-Hungarians. However, after the Serbs exerted mounting pressure throughout the night, they finally recaptured the town on August 19th. After several other decisive Serbian attacks along the front, Austro-Hungarian morale suddenly collapsed, as their army began a panicked and disorderly retreat all along the front line. The

WORLD WAR 1

Serbian High Command ordered the pursuit of the enemy, further adding to the panic that reigned throughout the Austro-Hungarian ranks. During their flight across the River Drina and back into Bosnia, many Austro-Hungarian soldiers drowned.

However, celebrations were short-lived. Deep down, everyone knew that Serbia could not possibly hope to stave off the enemy's offensives indefinitely. The Austro-Hungarians, although embarrassingly defeated, had superior manpower and armament, which became obvious in the following engagement: the Battle of Drina. Fought between September 6th and October 4th, 1914, it was a renewed and fiercer offensive by the Austro-Hungarians, which put the Serbian Army to the test. The Battle of Drina was a series of heavy clashes, all of which exacted a heavy toll on both the invaders and the defenders. In the end, the Serbs were forced into a series of retreats, falling far back after the capture of Valjevo, a significant Serbian town. Still, the Serbs chose to regroup and counter, leading to the Battle of Kolubara immediately afterward. It was fought between November 16th and December 15th, 1914.

The Serbs were forced to abandon Belgrade on November 29th, and it was promptly occupied by the Austro-Hungarians. However, the Serbian army opted for a daring and surprising counterattack along the entire front line. Once more, the Austro-Hungarians were taken aback and were unable to properly react and withstand the Serbian attacks. The Serbs liberated many of their cities and, eventually, their capital. The Battle of Kolubara was a decisive Serbian victory and another embarrassment for the Austro-Hungarians. So much was this a failure for their army that the Austro-Hungarian commander Oskar Potiorek was immediately relieved of command. The reason was "a most ignominious, rankling, and derisory defeat."

On the other hand, Serbia entered the spotlight. It drew the attention of correspondents all over the world, and many visitors from abroad entered the country, glorifying its fighting spirit. Nevertheless, the Serbs could not feel the happiness the others did: not only was this opening stage of the war costly in resources and manpower, but the winter also brought a debilitating typhus epidemic, which claimed hundreds of thousands of lives in Serbia. The situation worsened even further in 1915. The central powers, mainly Germany and Austria-Hungary, emphasized the importance of conquering Serbia: it was a vital route to the Ottoman Empire, and it could be crucial to the war's outcome. Thus, October 1915 saw a renewed series of offensives against the weakened Serbian army. The Germans and Austro-Hungarians pressed toward Belgrade, and it was clear that this time, victory for the Serbs was near impossible. And then, when the Bulgarians suddenly and surprisingly attacked the Serbs from the rear, the situation turned dire. Serbian armies were threatened with full encirclement and destruction, and that was reason enough for the Serbian High Command to order the Great Retreat.

Hundreds of thousands of Serbian soldiers and civilians fled south, attempting to reach the coast of the Adriatic Sea and the allied navies that awaited there. The retreat was an ordeal of immense proportions, one that became etched into the Serbian national memory as one of its greatest struggles. Hampered by the constant bad weather and near-impassable roads, the long columns of refugees suffered many casualties along the way. The retreat's most infamous portion occurred when the refugees traversed the inhospitable Albanian mountains. Their numbers were decimated by the freezing winter conditions and sporadic attacks by remote Albanian tribesmen. The Great Retreat claimed a staggering number of lives: over 160,000 civilians perished, and the army endured 77,455 dead and 77,278 missing.

WORLD WAR 1

Serbian airplane, 1915

Meanwhile, in the West, almost immediately after declaring war on France, Germany put into motion its long-standing invasion plan. The campaign began on August 4th, 1914, just a few days after Belgium announced that it would remain neutral in the event of war, and would deny free passage to Germany. The German plan for the conquest of France was created long before that. Known as the "Schlieffen Plan," after its creator, Field Marshal Graf Alfred Von Schlieffen, it was a strategic attempt to fool the French and outflank them. A similar approach was undertaken several decades later, in the Second World War.

The core of the Schlieffen plan was centered on a wide, sweeping flanking maneuver, by which they would bypass the core of the French army, capture Paris, and strike the enemy in the rear. This would trap the French Army and eliminate France from the war as soon as possible. Before the war commenced, the Germans appropriately deployed approximately 80% of their army toward the West and the French border. To achieve their plan, the Germans first invaded Luxembourg on August 2nd, 1914, violating its neutrality and rapidly sweeping through this small nation. It fell without any opposition. Just two days later, Belgium was attacked fiercely by the armies of Generals von Bülow and von Kluck. The next day, August 5th, saw the devastating Battle of Liège, which lasted until August 16th and ended in a victory for the Germans. Both sides suffered heavy casualties. Afterward, most of the Belgian army retreated, and Belgium was effectively conquered by August 23rd. During its occupation, numerous radical policies by the Germans were introduced, and many atrocities committed, in what was to become the so-called "Rape of Belgium."

After the German conquest of both Luxembourg and Belgium, they were ready to execute the next stage of the Schlieffen Plan. As planned, the German army entered northern France, where they faced the combined forces of France and the British Expeditionary Force. What followed was the Battle of the Frontiers, a series of intense clashes from August 7th to September 16th, 1914, that resulted in heavy losses on all sides. Some of the major battles fought in this period were the Battle of Charleroi and the Battle of Mons. As a direct consequence of the Battle of the Frontiers, Paris itself came under threat. This happened when the French Fifth Army, which had previously managed to delay the German advance, was almost completely annihilated by the German 1st and 2nd armies. Both the French and the British then commenced a full retreat and were pursued. Meanwhile, the French forces from the east managed to reach Paris and mount a defense of the capital. This resulted in the First Battle of the Marne.

At the Marne, the Germans managed to reach positions 70 kilometers outside of Paris. When the Germans encountered the British and French forces, the resulting battle became a decisive engagement that would dictate the fate of France. It lasted for six days and resulted in a full German retreat, ending their plans to conquer France. What happened next was crucial in the development of the Great War: the Germans retreated north across the River Aisne, and there, they dug in. This established the earliest outlines of the static, trench-oriented front line that would come to define the Western Front. Another attempt was made by the Germans to break the Allied forces and penetrate into France, resulting in the First Battle of Ypres, which ended in a stalemate and finally made it clear that their original plan was simply not going to work. The First Battle of Ypres was a costly affair for both the Germans and the Allies and clearly showcased the direction in which this war was heading. With more than 200,000 casualties, it was the first true insight into the brutality of this new global war.

The formation of the Western Front became the "iconic" representation of the First World War. The stalemate that ensued after those initial battles dictated the shape of the front between the Entente and the Central Powers, a frontier that wouldn't significantly change for the duration of the war. Those initial battles clearly determined that warfare had changed for good in the 20th century. : the old strategies of the 19th-century wars were simply not efficient anymore. This clash between the new and the old resulted in the emergence of attrition warfare, whereby the focus shifted toward mass use of artillery and machine guns and new military industries in order to wear out an enemy and establish supremacy on the ground and in the air. As a response to this, trench warfare emerged as the only efficient means of countering the artillery and protecting the infantry. Thus, it was that the huge parts of the western fronts were covered with elaborate networks of trenches, between which were huge expanses of no man's land. This warfare was especially costly in manpower. Relying on mass charges of the previous wars, officers sent thousands of men in blind charges or slow marches across this no man's land, where they would be easy pickings for new and advanced machine guns or long-range artillery.

Ruins of Carency, Western Front

By 1916, it became obvious that breakthroughs were a distant and somewhat unreachable objective. The Germans were the first to realize this, learning from their past experiences in 1914. By realizing the new consequences of modern warfare, the Germans opted for a new tactic: mass death. Yes, you read that right. The German command wanted to defeat France by sheer number of inflicted casualties. Their plan was to limit Allied provisions by targeting their supply lines, and then focusing on the French positions from which retreat was difficult. One such position they had in mind was the town of Verdun, which lay near the front lines and was strategically closed off. This was the idea of General Erich Von Falkenhayn, the Chief of German General Staff. He focused all his attention on Verdun, establishing air superiority to eliminate any threat from above, and conducting devastating artillery barrages.

What resulted was the infamous and widely known Battle of Verdun. In an attempt to weaken the defenders, Falkenhayn conducted eight hours of full artillery bombardment. The city itself was characterized by a series of ridges and fortifications that surrounded it, and the German command knew that they would be the crucial objectives to take if they were to win at Verdun. The battle began on February 21st, 1916, and initial fighting was marked by a rapid German advance. By the 28th, they captured the first key fortification and were halted by French reinforcements.

WORLD WAR 1

The next serious conflict was on the famed Dead Man's Hill (*Le Mort Homme*). This height was a key strategic objective for the Germans, as it defended the French artillery emplacements. Capturing it meant a key strategic victory against the French. This meant that some of the worst and chaotic fighting of the war was held right there.

The battles for Dead Man's Hill were devastating. The French artillery dominated the battlefield, inflicting heavy casualties. The Germans would manage to capture forward French trenches, but bombardment and counterattacks would drive them off. This back-and-forth fighting lasted for more than a month, and the whole landscape was soon transformed into a meld of craters, mud blood, and debris. It was one of the costliest engagements of the entire year. The Germans eventually captured the hill in late May 1916.

But over that summer, with the change in the French high command, France went on an offensive. Step by step, suffering heavy losses, the French managed to repulse the Germans with the aid of artillery, and eventually came out as the winners of the Battle of Verdun. It became known as the "Mincing Machine," and one of the most infamous engagements of the whole war. The

WORLD WAR 1

French suffered close to 355,000 casualties, and the Germans, 400,000.

The French were sorely pressed by their losses at Verdun. The Allied High Command attempted to alleviate the pressure on the French by planning a new offensive that would utilize mainly British forces. The plan involved attacking multiple points around the River Somme, alleviating the pressure on the French positions, and penetrating the German lines. Thus began the Battle of the Somme, on July 1st, 1916, when the British divisions, supported by minor French forces, attacked German trenches after several days of heavy rain. The heavy bombardment of the Germans by the British artillery was largely ineffective, and so, the British unknowingly marched toward a ready and largely unaffected German army. During the initial British assault, where they blindly marched and charged across the muddy ground, the casualties were appallingly high. The British suffered 57,000 casualties in a single day, the largest number in the history of the British Army.

The Somme was something of a testing ground, with the British changing their approach by attempting to apply lessons learned at Verdun. This prolonged the fighting, and the British aimed for

WORLD WAR 1

air superiority over the battlefield. In July and August, the British continued attacking, again with little to no success. In the very final stages of the battle, the British deployed even more divisions and, for the first time ever, introduced tanks into the fighting. Neither worked. By early November 1916, the Battle of the Somme was over and inconclusive. The British managed to gain just eight kilometers of ground, driving a bulge into the German salient, but nothing more than this. It could be argued that the Somme was either a draw or an Allied defeat. Either way, it came with a catastrophically high cost in lives lost. The British suffered a mind-numbing 420,000 casualties, while the French endured 200,000. The Germans experienced roughly 460,000 casualties. The Somme was one of the bloodiest battles of the Great War. And such an incredible number of casualties brings us to an all-important question, one that we cannot avoid:

What *was the human cost of the war?*

Chapter 3: The Human Cost of War

The First World War marked a dramatic departure from all previous conflicts; its unprecedented scale of destruction, industrialized methods of warfare, and prolonged duration resulted in a staggering human cost unlike anything that any country had ever witnessed before. The world had advanced quickly: the rigid linear tactics of the Napoleonic era, common just a century earlier, had become a thing of the past. Gone were the single-shot breech-loading rifles, smoothbore cannons, and sabre-wielding cavalry charges. In just a few decades, the world pushed forward into an age of grueling attrition warfare, of tanks, trucks, and machine guns, and into an era of warfare where artillery reigned uncontested. But nowhere was this horrific modern war felt more acutely than in the trenches, where common soldiers endured conditions that tested the limits of human endurance and left the world aghast. It is only when we stop and think about the soldiers' experiences in this war — the stories of their toils and trials — that we can truly understand how horrifying the

WORLD WAR 1

Great War really was. Because after all, these were young men, their lives only beginning in earnest. They had dreams, hopes, and aspirations; loved ones waiting back home; parents and siblings, wives and children, hoping for their return. But in the Great War, over 10 million servicemen, and a few women, never returned home. Today, their letters and diaries offer some of the most poignant insights into their daily lives, fears, hopes, and ultimate sacrifices.

WORLD WAR 1

Australian infantry wearing small box respirators (SBR). The soldiers were from the 45th Battalion, Australian 4th Division at Garter Point near Zonnebeke, Ypres sector, 27 September 1917.

For the men stationed along the Western Front, life in the trenches was a grim reality. Shelled by artillery, half-starved and suffering from various ailments, these men were required to wage war in horrid conditions. Letters from British, French, and German soldiers frequently speak of the mud, the rats, and the ever-present threat of death. Private Edward Henry Cecil Stewart served in the 1/5 Grenadier Company, London Rifle Brigade, and perished in combat on July 1st, 1916. One of the letters he sent home — possibly the last one he ever wrote — perfectly describes the horrendous conditions of the Western Front:

"... As long as you kept your head down you were comparatively safe, so as it went on, this was where I had my first escape. I was on sentry duty for a couple of hours, from 1am to 3am and was instructed to keep a sharp look out. I did not care for the idea of keeping my head above the trench and looking for beastly Germans, however it had to be done, it was quite uncanny to watch the enemy trench which appeared somewhat like a black wave and only sixty yards in front, then you would suddenly see the flash of their rifles and machine guns immediately after would come the report and nasty thuds on the sandbags which you might be resting against. I fired about five shots at their flashes (the only target to aim at) then another two shells which lodged in the parapet either side of my head leaving about 2 to 3 inches between me and certain death. I thought that near enough but it turned out that it was to have something nearer than that. Our casualties here amounted on the average, to about two per day killed, of course, we thought it terrible at the time at least I did.

WORLD WAR 1

Early April saw us relieved by another division and we were sent a few miles back for a well-earned rest, which consisted of physical drill and a run before breakfast. The remainder of the morning was spent in platoon drill musketry drills. After dinner we put the "cap on" our rest (why so called I do not know) by having a route march for two hours. We spent a few days like this and were dispatched with all possible speed to Ypres, here we went in to support the Canadians and spent a most unpleasant eight days, during which time we lost several hundred men, nearly all my friends who came out in the same draft and were killed or wounded, we had to retire, the best part being that the Germans did not find this out until two days after when we were more or less safely bivouacking in a very pretty wood. We stayed here for about a week; then we got to work again, digging reserve trenches just behind the front line, building up parapets which had been demolished by the enemy's high explosive shells and such like, working all night and getting what sleep we could in the daytime. One morning we were awakened by the most awful din, it seemed as though hell had broken loose, shells were falling like summer rain. And people have often told me in the course of conversation it was raining shells and I admit I took it with a grain of salt. It could not be possible I thought, but such I was surprised to find it was possible and actually taking place there about 3.30am. This bombardment started and about half an hour later, I, with three others, were ordered to start reinforcing. We went up in fours, it being considered safer that way, half a mile over open

WORLD WAR 1

ground we had to do, this being swept continually with shells, to give you a slight idea I can say the previous night, just in front of our reserve trenches was a beautifully green field, and the next morning it was as much as one could do to see any grass at all, simply one mass of craters, varying in diameter from ten to twelve paces."

— Letter from Private Edward Henry Cecil Stewart, 1/5 Grenadier Company, London Rifle Brigade. Believed to be written shortly before his death on July 1st, 1916. Reproduced here as a historical document presumed to be in the public domain.

This letter vividly illuminates the constant uncertainty of life in the trenches. Living in perpetual fear and seeing all your friends and squad mates perish was an undeniably horrifying experience. But for these soldiers, letters existed as a rare consolation. To be able to write to those waiting at home, and to express their emotions and fears, was nothing short of liberating, and gave them strength in times of difficulty. Richard Gilson, serving in France with the 4th Seaforth Highlanders, wrote to his mother on May 12th, 1915. His letter describes how gut-wrenching it was to see all the fellow soldiers he knew and grew close to die brutally in combat.

"My dear Mother,

WORLD WAR 1

"Have just come through a particularly nasty period. We went into the trenches on Wednesday night and on Sunday morning at 5am our Artillery commenced bombarding the German trenches and after 20 minutes had elapsed we went over the parapet. My goodness what a reception the Huns had in store for us, they simply swept the ground with machine gun fire and shrapnel. Poor old 'C' coy. caught it hot and Neuve Chapelle seemed to be a fleabite compared with this. It was found impossible to make any advance in our quarter, so I dug myself in and awaited events. It was horrible suspense, as I seemed to be the only man untouched, all around me, and being personally acquainted with each man made matters worse, in fact, it's all wrong to call them men, as they were mostly mere boys.

About early afternoon I was hailed from the trench as to whether it was possible for me to get back. I replied in the affirmative and decided to run the risk of getting potted on the way. So I commenced crawling on my stomach until about a few yards from the parapet, then made a spring and rushed headlong over the top, nearly spoiling the features of a few who happened to be in the trench and were not expecting me. We were relieved that afternoon, but some of the fellows did not get in until nightfall and they experienced another bombardment… Billy Hastings is quite fit and the only pal left. We have been resting since and getting information about the (illegible) but by all reports we shall be up again soon. No rest for the wicked it is said, and if true we must surely be a bad lot.

WORLD WAR 1

What a terrible thing about the Lusitania, and with so many Americans aboard. I should imagine there will be more trouble. I have received a box and letter dated 6th and am most thankful for everything you are all doing for me. (censored.)

As regards the pads, (masks of cotton pads which served as gas masks), all we were served out with were made 'on the spot' and consisted of a piece of gauze and tape and were steeped in a solution of bicarbonate of soda, prior to this charge. I lost all my belongings except the Gillette (razor) so should be glad of a few toilet requisites when next you are sending a parcel. Do not worry about the towel and perhaps Frank would get me a shaving brush. Must now close. Much love to all. From your affectionate son, Dick."

— *Letter from Richard Gilson, 4th Seaforth Highlanders, written to his mother on May 12th, 1915. Reproduced as a historical document presumed to be in the public domain.*

And then, there was the weather. The soldiers on the Western Front endured awful conditions, making matters much worse for them. Not only did they have to endure constant shelling, enemy charges, mounting casualties, and debilitating illnesses, but they had to do it all in constant rain and mud. This letter from Jonathan George Symons of the 13th County of London Regiment (King's Royal Rifles Corps) tells about horrible French weather late in the year.

WORLD WAR 1

"[...] At the present time we are in dugouts. The weather is simply awful, raining day after day and especially night after night... To tell you the truth, while writing this letter I am wet through to the skin and not a dry thing for a change. We have got our winter fur coats and gum boots, but the latter cause more curses than you can imagine, for instance last night I was sent off to select dugouts for our platoon, which is number 37. It was pitch dark, no light allowed and in a strange place, well honestly I fell over at least 20 times, got smothered in mud from head to feet and on the top of that wet though it rained in torrents. On a round of inspection this morning to see if all were 'comfortable' I was 'blinded' up hill and down dale, 'Sergeant this' and 'Sergeant that'.

How can you expect men to live in this, and then to put a dampener on the lot, was the language from the occupiers who unfortunately were in a residence that fell in during the night. They took shelter under a tree from 2am after looking for me for half an hour or so, but they could not find me, for the only thing that would shift me, after settling down, if I may call it that, would be a 'Jack Johnson' and then I would have no option.

While in the trenches last week John and I were up to our knees in water and got our gum boots half full. The line is a bit quiet lately and only now and again do we get a shelling, but one gets used to it. That, to give you an idea, is like sitting at Paddington and hearing the engines screech.

WORLD WAR 1

After our stretch this time I shall be looking forward for a short leave for I have been here nearly three months now and we stand a good chance. Well I must now conclude… Yours sincerely, Jack Symons"

— *Letter from Jonathan George "Jack" Symons, 13th County of London Regiment (King's Royal Rifle Corps). Written during late 1915 and reproduced here as a historical document presumed to be in the public domain.*

Of course, the suffering caused by the war was not limited to the trenches. The home front experienced its own share of hardship, sacrifice, and anguish. While soldiers fought on battlefields, civilians struggled to maintain normal life amid food shortages, air raids, and the loss of loved ones. In Britain, Germany, and France, rationing became a hallmark of civilian life. Food shortages were severe, particularly in Germany, where the Allied blockade led to the infamous "Turnip Winter" of 1916/1917, during which even basic staples became scarce. Diary entries from Berlin at that time recount children crying from hunger, long queues outside bakeries, and increasing reliance on substitute foods.

The Great War is often described as a "total war" because it profoundly impacted the populations of the nations involved, engulfing not only military forces but also entire civilian populations and national economies. Unlike previous conflicts, which primarily involved fighting on the battlefield, World War I saw the *complete* mobilization of nations. Governments directed their nations' resources toward the war effort, drawing all aspects of society, including civilians, into the conflict and its resultant hardships. Men were recruited into the army, women entered the workforce in unprecedented numbers, and civilians were forced to adjust to wartime restrictions, rationing, and other major challenges. As such, this "total war" concept blurred the line between the battlefield and the home front, as civilians were increasingly subjected to wartime pressures and privations. The war seeped into every corner of life, forcing many people to experience hardships that many of them had never experienced before.

Without a doubt, one of the most visible hardships on the home front was the severe shortage of food, fuel, and nearly all other essential goods. This was largely because the war effort demanded vast resources, which were often redirected from civilian use to military needs. In Britain, for example, the government established a Ministry of Food to oversee rationing, ensuring that food was distributed as fairly as possible to both military personnel and the civilian population. The British government introduced bread rationing as early as 1917, and by 1918, most basic foodstuffs — meat, butter, and sugar— were subject to government-imposed limits.

Britain was not the only one with such measures. The situation in Germany was even more dire, as the British naval blockade cut off imports of food and raw materials. By 1917, German civilians faced severe shortages, and Germany's population was severely malnourished. In the "Turnip Winter", the German people were forced to subsist on turnips, potatoes, and other root vegetables — foods that were often scarce and had previously been used primarily as cattle feed. This led to not only widespread physical hardship but also contributed to social unrest, as civilians became increasingly frustrated with deprivation and the government's failure to improve conditions. In France, civilian life was similarly disrupted. Areas close to the front lines endured immense suffering as the front shifted and the German army occupied large swathes of French territory. The French government relocated thousands of civilians from the war zone and implemented strict controls on supplies, transportation, and distribution. Despite these measures, the constant strain on resources led to widespread scarcity and inflation.

WORLD WAR 1

During the Great War, everyone was expected to step up and contribute to the war effort in service to their country. While men fought on the front lines, women played their own crucial role. The role of women on the home front during World War I marked a dramatic shift in societal expectations and gender roles. With millions of men enlisted in the military, women were increasingly called upon to take on roles traditionally reserved for men, a change that was particularly pronounced in industrialized nations such as Britain, France, and Germany.

In Britain, women stepped into jobs in munitions factories, filling positions as welders, machine operators, and engineers. The "*munitionettes*" (women employed in munitions factories) became an iconic symbol of wartime female labor. The government launched campaigns encouraging women to work, and women's employment rose dramatically during the war. In 1914, just 23% of women were employed in industrial roles; by 1918, that number had increased to over 30%.

"We are incomparably the greatest employers of women there has ever been in the world, we are the pioneers of women's employment in the industrial and even the military field. Whatever may be the future position which women's labour will take after the war, it will be enormously influenced by

WORLD WAR 1

the actual practice which has been followed when so much in the making, and when so much control is vested in the organisation of the Ministry of Munitions... Now is the time during the Great War for us to perceive, discover and proclaim the principles which should regulate, for perhaps the lifetime of a whole generation and perhaps for longer, the lines of advance on which women's industrial work should proceed."

—*Winston Churchill, 1917*

"The Munitions Girls" Stanhope Forbes

At the time, this marked an almost revolutionary shift in traditional gender roles that had persisted for centuries. Women felt empowered to take on duties previously reserved for men, ushering in a new era of female emancipation. For example, in France, women played a vital role in sustaining the economy while men were away at the front. Many women worked in factories that produced munitions, clothing, and other essential war supplies. However, this shift in gender roles was not without tension, as many men returned home from the front to find their jobs occupied by women. Despite the necessity of this new workforce, some men resented the presence of women in traditionally male-dominated industries, leading to social friction.

Women's involvement in the workforce during World War I not only proved their capabilities across a wide range of occupations but also served as a catalyst for the broader women's suffrage movement. In countries like Great Britain, women's contributions to the war effort helped solidify the case for granting them the right to vote, which they achieved in 1918. And then, there is nursing, arguably their most important contribution in the war. Female nurses played a critical role during the Great War, significantly contributing to the care of wounded soldiers and shaping the future of nursing as a modern profession. At the outbreak of the war, a tremendous number of women joined the nursing profession, driven by a sense of duty and patriotism. Initially, there were limited opportunities for women in medicine, but the war dramatically expanded their presence in the field.

Nurses worked under often harrowing conditions, providing medical care in makeshift field hospitals, military camps, and even on the front lines. They experienced the war's brutality together with the men, shoulder to shoulder. The British Royal Army Nursing Service (RANS) and the Voluntary Aid Detachments (VADs) were among the more prominent groups that mobilized women for wartime nursing. The VADs, for instance, were volunteers who not only provided medical care but also assisted with logistics, driving ambulances, and organizing supplies.

WORLD WAR 1

*The Red Cross during the First World War.
American nurses at a Red Cross hospital, Liverpool.*

Female nurses faced immense challenges. They dealt with the devastating effects of modern warfare, including managing wounds caused by new, unprecedented weapons like machine guns and gas. Many of them worked in areas where they were exposed to danger, with some even being combat casualties themselves. However, their efforts were instrumental in reducing soldiers' mortality rates and improving the overall effectiveness of military hospitals. Beyond medical care, their compassion provided a much-needed boost to morale during one of the most brutal and

WORLD WAR 1

traumatic periods in history. The gruesome experiences of these nurses are best understood from their letters. One such, dated 1917 and sent from France, states:

"[...] The front lines are no place for the faint-hearted. I cannot imagine the terror you must face in the trenches, for here, in this makeshift hospital that has become my home, the scenes are unspeakable. The constant hum of the distant artillery fire is ever-present, and the air is thick with the scent of earth and blood. You would think, by now, that one could grow accustomed to the constant suffering, but the truth is, I find myself in shock every single day. Our wards are filled with the wounded, the dying, and the broken. You cannot imagine the horrors that enter through those doors - men with limbs torn off, faces unrecognizable, their eyes staring blankly into the distance as if they have already left their bodies behind.

The hardest part, my dear, is seeing the hope drain from the soldiers as the days go by. We do our best to care for them, but there is so little that we can do. [...] "

— Anonymous nurse, letter from a field hospital in France, 1917. Reproduced as a historical document presumed to be in the public domain.

While civilians faced material shortages and labor demands, they also endured immense psychological and emotional strain. The frequent telegrams bearing news of frontline casualties created an atmosphere of constant anxiety. For Britain, the death toll was staggering. Over 700,000 British soldiers died during the conflict, and the impact was felt deeply within every community. In France, the toll was even higher, with over 1.3 million soldiers killed. In both countries, the grieving process was complicated by the fact that many of the dead were never fully accounted for, their bodies either lost on the battlefield or buried in unmarked graves.

The psychological toll on the civilian population was not limited to those who had lost family members; the war created a pervasive atmosphere of fear, loss, and uncertainty for everyone. The constant threat of bombing raids, particularly in cities like London, which was occasionally struck by German Zeppelins and bombers, added to the stress. In Germany, civilians lived in a state of fear of Allied air raids, which became more frequent in the later years of the war.

To make matters even more unbearable, families had to cope with the absence of their loved ones and the agonizing uncertainty about their fate at the front lines. And for those families fortunate enough to welcome their loved one's home, many had to face profound changes in the men they once knew, as soldiers returning from the front often brought with them physical and psychological scars. Shell shock, what we now know as post-traumatic stress disorder (PTSD), was a common affliction among returning soldiers, and it often strained families and communities. In many cases, they were entirely unrecognizable.

Stress and uncertainty were an everyday occurrence on the home front, even so far from the front lines and the trenches. The Great War marked the first use in history of large-scale aerial bombing. It introduced a new and terrifying aspect of modern warfare in which the civilian population became targets in unprecedented ways. Early in the war, the Germans introduced the Zeppelins — airships used for reconnaissance and bombing missions. They carried out numerous raids on Britain, terrorizing civilians and disrupting everyday life. As the war progressed, both sides began to use massive bombing attacks to damage cities, especially targeting those that had developed industries. By 1915, the German army began bombing civilian targets in France, including the capital city of Paris. The first large-scale bombing raid on London took place in 1917, and over the course of the war, both sides targeted civilian infrastructure, causing widespread fear and destruction. The bombings' psychological impact was profound. In cities such as Paris and London, civilians lived in near-constant fear of the next air raid. Early in the war, they were largely defenseless, as effective air defenses were still being developed, which only made their angst even worse. Londoners developed strategies for coping with their fear, such as gathering in underground stations during air raids. Even so, the constant bombing took its toll on civilian morale. In Germany, Allied bombing raids targeting cities such as Berlin and Hamburg caused immense destruction and loss of life. In addition to the human toll, there was a significant loss of culturally valuable items, with many of the world's most important paintings, sculptures, and books destroyed.

Another key aspect of life on the home front was *propaganda*. Governments worked hard to control the flow of information, keeping the public motivated and the war effort strong. Propaganda was used to maintain morale, encourage enlistment, and persuade civilians to support national goals and the ongoing war effort. In Britain, the Ministry of Information was responsible for creating and disseminating wartime propaganda, which painted a picture of the enemy as barbaric and profoundly evil, an enemy worth vanquishing by the noble and just Allied Powers.

WORLD WAR 1

The population was rallied through posters, newspapers, films, and fiery speeches, while information that might have lowered morale was heavily censored.

The censorship of war news was another significant aspect of civilian life during the conflict. The Allies controlled the flow of information, carefully managing reports from the front lines to prevent panic or disillusionment and the loss of morale. In Germany, censorship was also strict, with the government controlling news about military setbacks and minimizing reports about civilian suffering caused by the war.

Although most civilians were deeply committed to supporting the war effort, pockets of resistance and dissent emerged. In both the Central Powers and the Allied nations, anti-war sentiments grew as the conflict dragged on and casualties continued to rise. In Germany, the brutal realities of life on the home front sparked widespread unrest. Severe food shortages and civilian hardships fueled discontent, leading to strikes breaking out in major German cities. By 1918, protests demanding an end to the war had erupted in Berlin and other cities.

In Russia, the situation escalated even further. The war acted as a catalyst for the Russian Revolution of 1917, as civilians grew increasingly dissatisfied with the Tsarist regime's handling of the war and its disastrous impact on the Russian people. Like Germany, failure to end the war quickly, combined with economic hardship, led to widespread protests and strikes, culminating in the abdication of Tsar Nicholas II and the rise of the Bolsheviks.

The Great War was a fiery sword, but it had two edges. The war was quick to spill from the trenches and the front lines to the home front, seeping into the everyday lives of the entire populace. The soldiers faced grueling conditions, constant danger, and the possibility of a horrifying death. The civilian population, on the other hand, was forced to endure immense hardships that included rationing, shortages, fear, uncertainty, and, in some nations, even acts of violence such as rape and pillaging. Even so, the people were called upon to contribute to the war effort in new and unprecedented ways, as women entered the workforce in large numbers, and common people mobilized to support their fighting men in various ways.

Chapter 4:
Innovation, Destruction, and Healing

Today, the Great War is often remembered for all the wrong reasons — the staggering loss of life, the horrific conditions on the front lines, and a world grappling with collapsing empires, shifting borders, and the effects of modern warfare. Yet, innovation emerged from the crucible of war, sadly combined with *destruction*. The result was a world of stalemates, trench warfare, and relentless attrition — conditions that proved ideal for the development of new military technologies. These advancements would forever alter the nature of warfare with consequences that still resonate today, more than a century later. The war was marked by the introduction of three revolutionary new weapons: *tanks*, *poison gas*, and *airplanes*. They were innovations that were not only instrumental in shaping the course of the conflict, but also in laying the foundation for modern warfare. Each of these technologies represented a significant departure from traditional combat tactics, influencing the strategies employed on both the Western and

WORLD WAR 1

Eastern Fronts and impacting the post-war geopolitical landscape.

Arguably, the most revolutionary military invention of the Great War was the *tank* — a completely new concept that transformed the battlefield. While the idea of an armored vehicle capable of crossing difficult, muddy terrain and breaking through barbed wire and the enemy lines was not entirely new at the outset of the Great War, it was during this conflict that it became a battlefield reality. However, the tank's scale of use and its practicality as a weapon were only achieved once the war was in full swing. Early concepts of tanks came from thinkers such as J.F.C. Fuller and Lieutenant Colonel Ernest Swinton of the British Army, who recognized the need for a weapon on the Western Front that could cross the deadly barbed wire of no man's land and break through enemy defenses. So, the tank was developed in response to the stalemate caused by trench warfare and the practice of attrition warfare, which had left armies locked in static positions for months at a time. The British were the first to develop and deploy tanks, with the Mark I tank making its debut at the Battle of the Somme in 1916. The Mark I was a cumbersome and slow machine, weighing nearly 30 tons and capable of speeds of just three to four miles per hour. Despite its slow pace, the tank proved effective at traversing the battlefield's muddy terrain, crushing barbed wire, and giving the enemy troops a psychological shock. Although the Mark I's first combat deployment was far from a resounding success — many tanks broke down or became mired in the mud — it demonstrated mechanized warfare's potential.

A Big Tank Lumbering into action over a trench

Tanks were refined as the war progressed. The British introduced more advanced models, such as the Mark IV, which was more reliable and better protected by its armor. In 1917, the British Army launched the first large-scale tank offensive in the Battle of Cambrai. This marked a critical turning point in the development of tanks as a weapon of war. They proved capable of breaking through entrenched German defenses and opening gaps in enemy lines. However, success was short-lived due to difficulty in maintaining momentum and the German counterattacks that quickly followed. Nevertheless, the tank's potential as a breakthrough weapon was now undeniable. While the British were the primary innovators in tank development, the French and Germans also recognized the need for such a weapon. The French developed the Renault FT, which had a fully revolving turret and was smaller and more maneuverable. It would influence tank design for decades. The Germans, however, did not deploy tanks in large numbers during World War I, partly due to their focus on other technologies; however, they quickly developed tank tactics after the war, influencing future tank design. By the end of World War I, the tank had become a symbol of modern warfare, and its future combat role had been firmly established. Though initially viewed with skepticism, the tank's success in the war led to its widespread adoption in future conflicts, from World War II to the present day.

Alas, the war was a laboratory for the most gruesome and diabolical inventions, the tank being among the least terrifying. Far more insidious weapons were developed, with poison gas standing out as the most horrifying of them all. The use of chemical warfare was an unprecedented method of waging war, and it represented a major departure from the weaponry previously seen on the battlefield. It was meant to break the deadlock and the attrition of trench warfare, and cause mass panic, confusion, and casualties among the enemy. The first true large-scale use of chemical weapons occurred on April 22nd, 1915, during the Second Battle of Ypres, when the German Army released massive quantities of chlorine gas against French and Canadian forces. Soldiers came to dread this infernal weapon, as it caused suffocation, severe lung irritation, blindness, and ultimately horrible injuries and painful death.

The use of poison gas evolved throughout the war. At first, chlorine gas was used, which was effective in initial assaults, but it had limited "persistence" and was vulnerable to countermeasures, such as simple gas masks. This called for the invention of an even more diabolical weapon: *phosgene gas*. As an even deadlier option, phosgene gas could take up to 48 hours to fully show its effects, causing delayed reactions among its victims. Additionally, the Germans also utilized chloropicrin and diphosgene, which would cause severe lung damage and blindness, respectively.

WORLD WAR 1

One of the most notorious poison gas weapons was "mustard gas." First used by the Germans in 1917, it was a particularly horrifying agent as it caused blistering of the eyes, skin, and respiratory system. In contrast to the other gases, mustard gas could be absorbed through the skin, which made gas masks largely useless. As a result, it was the cause of significant long-term injuries and considerable suffering to many soldiers on the battlefield.

WORLD WAR 1

Type of gas mask used by the English to protect men and horses.

The Allies did not sit idly by; they responded by creating their own chemical weapons to combat the growing threat from the Germans. Even though chemical weapons were initially effective, their use posed significant logistical challenges. Wind was a critical factor in determining the range and movement of large poison gas clouds; sudden shifts in the wind could cause the gas to move back toward the user, potentially harming their forces. The use of gas also led to the development of defensive measures, such as the gas mask, which became standard issue for soldiers on both sides of the conflict. Countermeasures, however, did little to reduce gas warfare's psychological impact, as soldiers lived in constant fear of a gas attack. Gas attacks were often followed by artillery bombardments, making them even deadlier. By the war's end, chemical warfare caused an estimated 90,000 deaths and over one million wounded, which cemented their infamous reputation as brutal weapons of war. But even so, the use of gas was not enough to break the stalemate and attrition of trench warfare. The victims of chemical warfare did not live to see its eventual prohibition. The world was horrified by the use of such inhuman weapons, leading to their eventual ban in 1925, with the signing of the Geneva Protocol.

Another groundbreaking weapon introduced during the Great War was the airplane. This was the first major conflict that saw the widespread use of airplanes in combat. At just over a decade old, airplanes were still a recent invention. The war accelerated their development and deployment. In no time, they were transformed from simple reconnaissance tools into potent offensive weapons. At the start of the war, planes were used primarily for observation and mapping enemy positions, quickly proving valuable for intelligence gathering. However, as the war and airplane technology progressed, pilots inevitably engaged in aerial combat. The first recorded instance of aerial combat took place in 1914, when a Serbian pilot, Miodrag Tomić, exchanged pistol shots with an Austro-Hungarian aviator over Western Serbia. In the months and years that followed, aerial combat (dogfights) became increasingly common in the skies over Europe.

BE 2c 90hp RAF 1A engine in flight.

It soon became clear that airplanes needed to be armed and their role redefined. The development of fighter aircraft was driven by the growing need for air superiority. The British and French developed popular and successful planes, such as the Sopwith Camel and the Nieuport 17. Both planes were equipped with special synchronized machine guns, which allowed the pilots to fire without hitting the spinning propeller at the front of the aircraft. In response, the Germans developed the famed Fokker Eindecker, which introduced the concept of synchronization gear that further enhanced the pilot's ability to shoot through the propeller. The earliest years of aerial combat were marked by these technological innovations, with pilots engaging in dogfights that were thrilling and often deadly.

As the war continued, the role of airplanes evolved beyond simple fighting. Larger planes were developed with the intent of bombing enemy cities and strategic infrastructure, chiefly railways and factories. While both the Germans and the British developed long-range bombers, their payload was somewhat limited (compared to aircraft that would appear in the Second World War). They were also quite vulnerable to enemy fighters and so required a heavy escort to successfully complete their missions. Even so, these early bombers foreshadowed the strategic bombing campaigns that would become a hallmark of future wars.

WORLD WAR 1

Of course, aircraft development during World War I was not limited to military applications. The war saw the first use of planes for aerial reconnaissance, mapping, and artillery spotting. Directing artillery fire from the air revolutionized the war's battlefield tactics. However, while airplanes had a significant psychological impact on both soldiers and civilians, their overall influence on the war's outcome was limited. The skies remained a battleground secondary to the trenches, with aircraft playing a supporting rather than decisive role. The technological advancements made during the war laid the groundwork for the development of modern air forces, and the role of airplanes in warfare would expand exponentially in the years to come.

Sadly, most of the innovations in the Great War were born from death and destruction. Yet, amid the devastation, people recognized that the need for healing was greater than ever. The conflict's unprecedented scale and brutality demanded transformative medical innovation, pushing the boundaries of healthcare in ways previously unimagined. In this way, the Great War, through its horrors, helped usher in a new era of medicine that affected both military and civilian life.

WORLD WAR 1

The trajectory of healthcare was forever altered by this war, as the enormous number of casualties — driven by mass charges and attrition warfare — placed overwhelming demands on the medical profession. However, the nature of the injuries sustained in this new type of warfare had never been seen before. After all, everything about this war was relatively new: machine guns, tanks, poison gas, airplanes, snipers, barbed wire, and just about every other instrument of destruction. These were weapons that all caused horrific wounds, such as deep shrapnel injuries, total blindness, severe gas poisoning, and extensive burns, all of which strained the limits of the medical knowledge and treatment methods that existed at the time.

One of the most significant challenges facing medical professionals during World War I was the treatment of wounds caused by shrapnel and explosive shells. Unlike in earlier wars, where battlefield wounds came from slower-moving projectiles like arrows, swords, or musket balls, the high velocity of shrapnel and the widespread use of artillery shells produced wounds that were deep, massive, and often contaminated with dirt, metal, and bacteria. Infection became a critical concern, as open wounds were exposed to unsanitary conditions in the trenches. As a result, medical professionals had to find innovative ways to deal with both the immediate trauma of these injuries and the long-term complications caused by infection.

One of the most significant medical advancements during this time was the refinement of surgical techniques. Prior to the war, field medicine was still largely inadequate. However, at the onset of the Great War, surgeons were confronted with new and complex types of injuries, forcing rapid innovation and adaptation. Treating these injuries and ensuring effective care demanded highly specialized and inventive approaches. During the war, antiseptic techniques — pioneered by British surgeon Sir Joseph Lister — were introduced and became widely adopted. This revolutionized wound treatment, especially on the front lines, and dramatically reduced the number of deaths from infection. However, the filthy and unhygienic conditions in the trenches meant antiseptics were not always enough. In order to improve survival rates, surgeons had to develop new and innovative treatment methods.

Plenty of these new treatment methods dealt with amputations, which were prevalent due to the horrid nature of this war. Even in the beginning stages of World War I, it became apparent that severely wounded limbs (which were a common occurrence) had to be amputated to ensure the potential survival of the wounded. As a result, specialized instruments and techniques for removing limbs were refined, and prosthetic limbs were greatly improved. These advances were mostly due to the input from medical professionals who worked directly with patients. The development of more functional prostheses, including the first attempts at artificial arms and legs with movable joints, revolutionized the rehabilitation process for soldiers. In many ways, this new (and somewhat morbid) dimension of the Great War foreshadowed the modern wars we see erupting across the globe today. In those dark years, artillery reigned on the battlefield, leaving soldiers maimed and scarred for life. Today, things have progressed to all-new heights of infernal warfare. Drones, remotely controlled and hard to destroy, are targeting soldiers and leaving them scarred for life equally to those who fought in the trenches. Is this another lesson we can learn from history? A lesson that tells us that war never changes, but only gains deeper and more horrifying dimensions?

The devastation wrought by artillery fire and the risk of death and mutilation were daily features of life for many soldiers on the front line. Lancashire Fusilier Bert Fearns wrote in his diary the

WORLD WAR 1

devastating consequences of a failed charge at the Battle of Poelcappelle in 1917.

"We were surprised that there wasn't as much machine gun fire as we expected but we did go through – it's difficult for me to say how big the area was, but I'd say it was about possibly 100 yards by 100 yards – and there was a mass of our fellows had been caught by low exploding shrapnel and they'd been absolutely slaughtered. It was the first time I smelt human blood – fresh – and it's the most horrible smell I've ever smelt. But they were lying there all over the place, just mutilated. We just had to keep going on and it's just as well we did as it could have unnerved us if we'd been too long in that place. I've never forgotten it..."

— Bert Fearns, Lancashire Fusiliers. Recollection of the Battle of Poelcappelle, 1917. Source unconfirmed, reproduced under fair use for educational and historical commentary.

As the war progressed, the "industries" that advanced the most involved weaponry and medicine — two sides of the same coin known as *war*. One sought to destroy, while the other aimed to save. It was a profound paradox, but such is the nature of warfare. Regarding medical innovations, one of the most important in the Great War was blood transfusion. While blood transfusions had been practiced for decades before the war, they were often unreliable, with transfused blood often rejected by the recipient's body. However, the sheer scale of bodily trauma during the war, especially in the form of extreme blood loss from shrapnel wounds and other injuries, made blood transfusions a crucial component of battlefield medicine. The first successful blood transfusions in the war were performed using blood obtained directly from the donor. However, the need for a more reliable system for storing and transporting blood quickly led to the development of blood banks. In 1917, American surgeon Dr. Oswald Hope Robertson established the first blood bank at the front.

This was a major leap in contemporary battlefield medicine, Blood could be collected, stored, and transported to where it was sorely needed, ensuring that soldiers in critical condition received blood promptly, giving them a greater chance of survival. Moreover, this development ushered in the start of modern blood donation systems, which would later become integral to medical practices worldwide.

The Great War was also a major turning point in the global fight against infectious diseases. On the battlefield, soldiers faced unsanitary and unhygienic conditions in crowded trenches, which accelerated the spread of illnesses. The most infamous of these diseases was the Spanish flu, which emerged in 1918 and infected millions of people worldwide. In fact, the Spanish flu caused more deaths than the war itself. Battlefield circumstances drove major advances in combating disease. Vaccines were used in great numbers, especially the vaccine for typhoid fever, which became a standard part of military medical protocol. Typhoid fever had been a serious concern in the trenches, where soldiers were exposed to contaminated food and water. The mass immunization campaigns undertaken during the war played a significant role in reducing the impact of this disease. Why this was such a major breakthrough is evident from the obvious importance of vaccination in our day and age.

In addition to vaccines, there was an increased focus on hygiene and sanitation. Medical professionals began to recognize the importance of preventing infections before they occurred. The introduction of more effective sterilization methods, including the widespread use of disinfectants and the boiling of surgical instruments, became essential practices that were later adopted by civilian hospitals and clinics. Additionally, World War I fostered the growth of the pharmaceutical industry, as the demand for treatments to combat bacterial infections, such as those seen in soldiers with infected wounds and gangrene, led to the development of more effective antibiotics. Although the discovery of penicillin would not occur until the 1920s, World War I accelerated the search for treatments to manage and control infections, which would become a central focus of medical research in the post-war years.

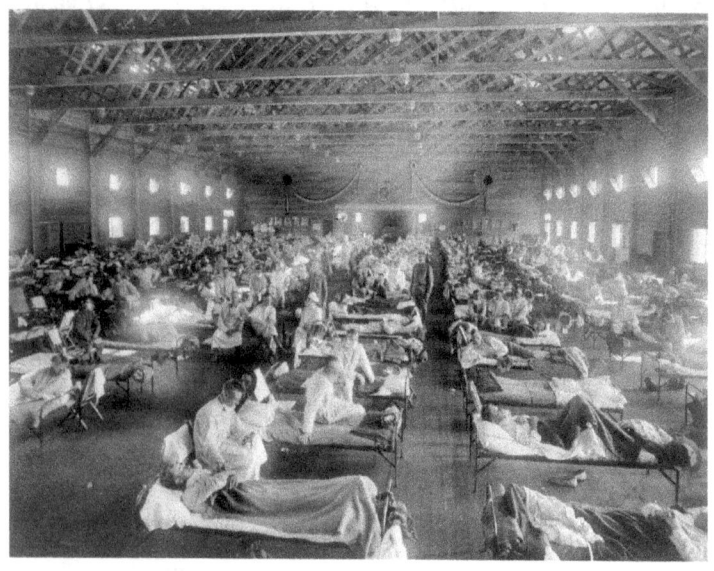

Emergency hospital during the Spanish Flu epidemic

Another significant medical breakthrough during the Great War was the recognition and treatment of psychological trauma, especially in those soldiers who had endured the horrors of battle. "Shell shock" — a term used to describe the psychological damage caused by relentless artillery bombardment — became a central issue for military medicine during the war. The symptoms of shell shock, which included tremors, paralysis, and psychological distress, were initially misunderstood and often stigmatized as cowardice or malingering. But as the war went on, medical professionals began to understand that these symptoms were not just the result of fear or stress but stemmed from actual psychological damage caused by constant exposure to violence, unrelenting stress, and horrifying realities of war. Psychiatrists like Dr. William Rivers, who treated soldiers at Craiglockhart War Hospital in Scotland, made significant advances in understanding and treating shell shock. Rivers and his colleagues pioneered therapeutic methods such as talk therapy and reconditioning exercises to help soldiers heal from their psychological wounds. The treatment of shell shock laid the groundwork for the development of modern psychiatry and trauma care. The recognition of psychological injuries as legitimate medical conditions paved the way for future developments in the treatment of PTSD and other mental health conditions, both in military and civilian contexts.

Chapter 5: The Spread of War

Noticeably different from the Western theater was the so-called Eastern Front. Differences in its geography, borders, and combatants made the Eastern Front a markedly different experience than the trench warfare of the Western Front. The Eastern Front stretched from the Baltic coast in the north, all the way to the Black Sea in the south, and included significant parts of Central Europe as well. It involved the Allied powers on one side — the Russians and the Romanians, with limited support from France, Britain, and Serbia; and the Central Powers on the other — the Ottoman Empire, Austria-Hungary, Bulgaria, and Germany.

In the broader historiography of the First World War, the Eastern Front is largely overlooked and misrepresented. Winston Churchill famously referred to it in the post-war years when he coined the term "unknown war." While the world's attention was focused on the devastation in the West, the East was embroiled in its own tragedies and fierce fighting. But it was not a war of attrition and stalemate, and mass death, compared to the Western Front. The Eastern Front's war was one of movement and maneuvering, of breakthroughs and new methods of warfare. It was a conflict that pitted two giant empires and their allies against one another: Russia and Austria-Hungary.

At the start of the war, Russia stepped in to support its little cousin Serbia. This decision was driven by a Pan-Slavic sense of awakening, and the Russian Tsar and his people felt obliged to assist their Slavic brethren. However, it was not all pride and brotherly love: Russia hoped to achieve sizable gains through the conflict, especially on the Black Sea coast, which was rich in resources. Moreover, it was obligated by its alliance to France, which was confronting the formidable power of Germany. Known as the "brooding bear" and the "giant of Europe," Russia had an army of nearly 3.5 million men upon full mobilization. In the north of the Eastern Front, it was facing the German 8th Army in Prussia, and further south were the Austro-Hungarian forces.

The Russian plan of attack was relatively straightforward; it was known as "Mobilization Schedule 19," by which two Russian Armies comprising a total of 29 infantry divisions, would be sent north in order to invade East Prussia. At the same time, the other half of their forces — consisting of four armies totalling 45 infantry divisions — would shift south and engage the Austro-Hungarians. This was a shrewd and sound tactical approach. It allowed Russia to answer the mounting pressures from the French High Command to become involved in Prussia and quickly defeat the Germans in the East while they were focused on the conflict in the West.

Russian troops going to the front line

Of course, the Austro-Hungarians and the Germans had anticipated Russia's strategy. As a result, there was a lot of maneuvering around the front, as both the Russians and the Austrians anticipated each other's next move. The first conflict on the Eastern Front occurred on August 23rd near the town of Krasnik, when the Austro-Hungarian 1st Army, commanded by General

Viktor Dankl, met the Russian 4th Army under the command of Baron von Saltza. The fighting was characterized by Austro-Hungarian frontal charges, which repulsed the Russians. The Austro-Hungarians won, but not without incurring an almost 50% casualty rate. Two days later, the Austro-Hungarian 4th Army and the Russian 5th Army fought a similar engagement at Komarow, which the Austro-Hungarians also won.

The Austro-Hungarians attempted to capitalize on their victories, but were unable to do so, as they had to shift eastward in response to the pending Russian invasion of Galicia. Subsequently, they suffered a devastating defeat at the famous Battle of Gnila Lipa, which took place from August 26th to 30th, 1914. The battle was fought between the Russian 8th and 3rd armies, commanded by Generals Brusilov and Ruzki, respectively, and the Austro-Hungarian 3rd Army under General Brudermann. The Russian victory was utterly decisive: their losses were meager compared to the several thousand Austro-Hungarian casualties. The latter's forces were forced into full retreat. General Brusilov's army took advantage of this victory and managed to capture the Lviv fortress (in Lemberg) on September 3rd — a part of the wider Battle of Galicia.

This achievement was followed by further Russian success. The Russian Cossack cavalry, which was a highly effective fighting force during the war, discovered a major gap between the positions of Austria's 1st and 4th armies, a crucial strategic advantage that was quickly exploited by the Russians. The commander of Russia's Southwestern Front, General Ivanov, sent his 5th and 9th armies through the gap and engaged the Austro-Hungarians in the Battle of Rawa-Ruska on September 3rd. Once more, they utterly defeated the Austro-Hungarians, inflicting 60,000 casualties. From there, they proceeded to the Austro-Hungarian stronghold of Przemyśl, to which they laid siege. The siege would last for 133 days and would end in a crushing and humiliating defeat for the Austro-Hungarians.

World War I's Eastern Front shrank in 1917, but it remained strategically important because it kept the Central Powers' forces divided. However, Russia was increasingly hampered by its deteriorating internal affairs. The rise of the Bolsheviks and the continual domestic crisis culminated in a significant change in the trajectory of Russia's history. Led by Vladimir Lenin and a cadre of other Jews, the Bolsheviks took over power in Russia on November 1st, 1917, greatly altering the future of the war in the East. Promptly after their rise to power, Russia descended into a bloody civil war, which would rage for three years. It was followed by a wave of fighting, massacres, and famines, resulting in countless deaths. The Eastern Front ceased to exist after the Treaty of Brest-Litovsk in 1918, allowing the Central Powers to shift their full attention to the Western Front.

But it was the Eastern Front that comprised another major facet of the First World War. It defined the mentality of the Slavic Russian people and their selfless sacrifices in the battles of this great conflict. Sheer numbers were their advantage, one that their generals eagerly exploited, often at too high a cost in human lives. Similar tactics would be repeated in the Second World War, when the suffering of this nation would reach all-new heights. So let it not be forgotten how bravely lives were laid down on all sides: both friend and foe fought bitterly to the very end. Sadly, all this fighting, this whirlwind of war and hate, engulfed civilians across Eastern and Central Europe. It is their sacrifices, too, that cannot be forgotten.

An equally important aspect of the Great War was its Pacific Theater. With the entry of New Zealand and Australia into the war, conflict soon engulfed Asia and the Pacific, where both the Allies and the Germans had colonial possessions. Although not as devastating as some other theaters, it was nonetheless quite significant and had a large influence on the latter outcome of the war. Fighting in the Pacific started on August 3rd, 1914, and lasted until January 5th, 1919. The focus of the Asian and Pacific Theatres was on naval warfare and the supremacy over the seas, all the while targeting German colonial possessions. Most engagements during this four-and-a-half-year period were bloodless, with only a few causing moderate casualties. Of all the engagements, though, the most significant was the Siege of the Chinese port of Tsingtao, then in German hands.

Due to the vast distances and scattered colonies in the Pacific, securing naval supremacy was the primary objective for all parties involved. By controlling major trade routes and blockading and besieging ports, a nation could gain a significant advantage over its enemy.

As mentioned, the Siege of Tsingtao (now Qingdao) was the defining engagement in this theatre of war. It was a port of significant strategic importance to the Germans. The Germans had a modest military presence consisting of approximately 4,000 troops, which were concentrated within an extensive network of fortifications, trenches, and coastal batteries.

German auxiliary cruiser SMS Seeadler,

Before the siege, Germany was faced with an ultimatum from Japan demanding the immediate withdrawal of German naval forces from Chinese and Japanese waters and the abandonment of the

WORLD WAR 1

Tsingtao port. Japan entered the Great War in 1914 on the Allied side, aiming to capitalize on Germany's unfavorable strategic position and expand its influence and territories in Asia. Germany's refusal of the ultimatum meant that an attack on Tsingtao was inevitable, and the German defenders were determined to be prepared for it.

Eager to claim the port and assert their dominance in the region, the Japanese sent five battleships, two battle cruisers, two destroyers, and one aircraft carrier — nearly their entire fleet. Furthermore, they sent a contingent of 23,000 soldiers, giving them a significant advantage over the defending Germans. The Japanese forces were further bolstered by aid from the British and the Chinese, both of whom sent several thousand additional troops.

Compared to these overwhelming numbers, the German garrison totalled just 3,625 soldiers, which was the entirety of Germany's East Asian Detachment. They were supported by a small naval force: four light gunboats, a single protected cruiser, and a single S90 torpedo boat. Despite being outnumbered, the German vessels were moderately successful early in the conflict: the torpedo boat managed to inflict heavy damage on HMS Kennet, a British Royal Navy destroyer, while the gunboat Jaguar managed to sink the Japanese destroyer Sarotaye. The torpedo boat later inflicted another heavy loss for the Japanese navy by sneaking out of the harbor and sinking the protected cruiser Takachiho, claiming 271 lives.

The Siege of Tsingtao began officially on October 31st with the first bombardment of the German fortifications. The German positions experienced constant shelling, day and night, for seven days. The Germans were only able to respond with moderate counter-fire until they ran out of ammunition on November 6th. Subsequently, the Japanese soldiers overwhelmed the shore defenses by attacking in successive waves. The following day, November 7th, saw the official end of the Siege of Tsingtao with the surrender of the German commanders. Over 3,500 German soldiers were taken prisoner. German casualties amounted to 199 dead and 503 wounded. For the Allied forces, these numbers were somewhat higher: 727 men were killed, and 1,335 were wounded. The Siege of Tsingtao was also the site of the first aerial victory in aviation history. The Germans had a single Taube airplane in their possession, which was flown successfully during the siege, and its pilot downed a Japanese Farman plane with nothing but his pistol.

WORLD WAR 1

In many ways, the Siege of Tsingtao is a very underrepresented part of the Great War and is often dismissed as insignificant, even though it had a major role to play in the bigger picture.

As the first true *global* war, World War I inevitably spread to Africa, where Germany, Britain, France, and other powers had established colonies. This became the stage for the African Theatre, a series of campaigns fought across the African continent from August 1914 to November 1918. Several campaigns were centered on the North African region and were initiated by the Ottoman and German Empires, both of which had territories there. Moreover, almost all the major powers of Western Europe had African colonies, which quickly became embroiled in the war.

Not only were the European colonies a source of manpower for the war, but they were also a rich source of raw materials needed to fuel Europe's industries in support of the war effort. As such, the African continent was an important honeypot for the empires of Europe, which wanted to exploit its every advantage. Africa was rich in gold, iron, sugar, silver, cocoa, petroleum, and other crucial resources. And in the few years of competitive tensions leading up to the war's outbreak, gaining and retaining supremacy of these colonies was imperative for Europe's major powers.

In 1914, the German Empire's colonies in Africa were: German West Africa (i.e., Kamerun, Neukamerun, and Togoland), German East Africa, and German South West Africa. These expansive, resource-rich territories were enormous in terms of square mileage. Many of them were several times larger than some contemporary European nations. These colonies later became the modern African nations of Togo, Burundi, Tanzania, Namibia, Rwanda, and Cameroon, as well as parts of Chad, Mozambique, Nigeria, Congo, Ghana, and others.

France, on the other hand, had significantly larger colonial territories, almost dwarfing those occupied by Germany. France's territories were collectively referred to as the French Colonial Empire, through which France had overlordship over many nations and regions in Africa, Asia, the Caribbean, and the Americas. Africa was expansive and France held control over numerous territories that included the Ivory Coast, French Sudan, Dahomey, Senegal, Niger, Mauritania, Upper Volta (now Burkina Faso), Guinea, Gabon, Cameroon, and others.

As for Britain, it possessed a vast, far-reaching colonial empire. exemplified by one of its most famous territories: the British Raj, or the British rule of India, which lasted from 1858 to 1947. India aside, the extent of Britain's African holdings was considerable. British West Africa consisted of the Gold Coast (modern-day Ghana), Gambia, Nigeria, South Cameroon, and Sierra Leone. And in British South Africa, there were Rhodesia, South Africa, Malawi, Botswana, and several others. The number of territorial holdings meant certain conflict for these European nations, and the quick emergence of the African Theatre would prove that correct.

German trenches in German Cameroon

WORLD WAR 1

One of the very first conflicts to break out on African soil was the North African Zaian War. It commenced nearly seven years after the start of the lengthy French conquest of Morocco. The main opposition during the conquest was the so-called Zaian Confederation, made up of various Berber tribes. Matters quickly escalated into a war with the French. The Great War escalated the conflict even further. France had to make significant cuts to their military presence in Morocco. The Central Powers, Germany especially, sought to capitalize on the situation by aiding the Zaian Confederation. Even so, the French managed to keep a foothold in Morocco, since the war with the Berbers was mostly one of repeated skirmishes and light raids. The Zaian War continued even after the First World War ended, lasting until 1921 and ending with a decisive French victory. Nonetheless, the Berber tribes continued a guerilla war against the occupation well into the 1930s.

Placing even more stress on France's colonial rule during their struggle in mainland Europe was the Volta-Bani War — an anti-colonial revolt that came as a surprise to the French. It spread out from uprisings in modern-day Mali and Burkina Faso, where local indigenous tribes banded together, chiefly the Bobo, Nuni, Bwa, and Lela peoples. What started as a localized uprising soon escalated into a full-blown war, with local populations mustering considerable forces across multiple fronts. The war lasted from 1915 to 1917 and delivered several serious setbacks to French rule in the region. The rebels organized two suppressive campaigns, both of which were a failure against the modern French colonial army. The Volta-Bani War was a sobering warning for the French. Even though they suppressed the Volta-Bani uprising, they created the colony of Upper Volta as the direct result of the administrative challenges caused by this conflict.

The war in Africa progressed even further with the onset of the British Kamerun Campaign. Its aim was to further weaken German colonial rule in Central and Western Africa. The territory of German Kamerun was invaded by a combined Allied force of British, French, and Belgian troops in August 1914. The fighting lasted until 1916, almost two full years. When the entire African theatre is considered, the Kamerun campaign resulted in significant casualties on both sides, but the German total was significantly higher. From the beginning, the Germans were both outnumbered and surrounded, since the territory of Kamerun was bracketed on all sides by Allied colonies. The entire campaign was marked by a series of sieges, skirmishes, and full-fledged battles, all stemming from Allied offensives.

The most significant of these engagements were the First and Second Battles of Garua in 1914 and 1915. Centered on the port city of Garua, they were a British effort to dislodge the entrenched and fortified German forces. The first battle ended in a decisive German victory, with the British unable to break through the defenses and suffering heavy casualties, including the loss of their entire officer corps.

The Germans sought to exploit their victory by conducting several offensives into British Nigeria, much to the dismay of the British command. The British eventually pushed the Germans back. Afterward, the British and French aimed to permanently eliminate the German fortifications at Garua. But in the meantime, the Germans had heavily dug in, creating a system of trenches and forts that could easily withstand a frontal assault. For that reason, the British opted for a siege. They created counter-trenches and conducted sapping and mining operations that gradually weakened the defending German garrison. They then opted to conduct a naval bombardment of the garrison, which inflicted a great number of casualties and prompted the Germans to surrender Gaura unconditionally. After enduring a series of defeats from Allied forces advancing from all sides, the German commander, led by Schutztruppe Commander Carl Heinrich Zimmerman, recognized that the Kamerun Campaign was lost. He ordered a full retreat, and all remaining German troops were extracted from the region.

Things fared no better on the eastern portion of the African continent. Among the most important operations conducted there was East African Campaign, centered on the Deutsch-Ostafrika region, which later spread like wildfire to neighboring colonies. It was also one of the longest fought on African soil, lasting from August 3rd, 1914, all the way to November 25th, 1918. Furthermore, the campaign was perhaps the most costly engagement in the African Theatre, as all parties involved suffered very high casualties.

At the time, the German Colonial Forces were headed by Lieutenant Colonel Paul Von Lettow-Vorbeck, better known as the "Lion of Africa" (*Der Löwe von Afrika*).He would acquire legendary status for his achievements in Africa during the Great War. His chief objective, and the one on which he based his strategy, was to divert the focus of the Allied forces from the Western Front in Europe to Africa.

WORLD WAR 1

Of the German troops in Africa, the largest portion was situated in the east (in German East Africa). However, they were greatly outnumbered by the combined forces of the Allies. Von Lettow aimed to provoke the Allies into invading Deutsch-Ostafrika so he could engage in a protracted defensive war. The German positions also threatened the Ugandan Railway, which was an important asset for the British. They also posed a significant threat to the neighboring Belgian colony of Congo.

The conflict in East Africa began in earnest on August 5th, 1914, when British forces of the Uganda Protectorate attacked German positions on Lake Victoria. The opening stages of the campaign were troubled by great confusion on both sides. Three days later, British navy cruisers shelled the German wireless station at Dar-es-Salaam. Von Lettow then focused his attention on defending the key strategic port city of Tanga, which the British intended to assault from the sea. At the resulting Battle of Tanga, Von Lettow and his German troops were outnumbered eight to one — an overwhelming disadvantage. But even so, the defenders under the command of the "Lion of Africa" successfully repelled the British attackers, securing a complete and decisive victory.

WORLD WAR 1

At the same time, the Battle of Kilimanjaro was underway. Fought concurrently with the Battle of Tanga, British Brigadier-General Aitken planned to invade and seize German East Africa with a swift and decisive offensive. Here, too, the German forces were outnumbered, this time four to one. And yet again, they completely defeated the British. In the wake of their two victories, Von Lettow's troops gained significant supplies, weapons, and ammo from the retreating British troops.

Thus, it was that the "*Löwe von Afrika*" managed to fight off the 300,000 men in the Allied armies with his outnumbered contingent of just 14,000 troops, of which only 3,000 were German *Schutztruppen (their colonial forces)*, and the rest local African tribal warriors. He led "the greatest single guerrilla campaign in history, and the most successful", and remained undefeated in the field. He was the only German commander who successfully invaded a part of the British Empire during the Great War.

WORLD WAR 1

Paul von Lettow-Vorbeck, Lion of Africa

WORLD WAR 1

Germany's hold on its African territories was fragile at the start of the war. Von Lettow's success in East Africa was perhaps the only major German achievement in the African Theatre. The continent and its colonies posed a string of challenges: the territories were extremely large, and the forces that occupied them were few and far between.

The German South West Africa colony was lost in 1915, German Kamerun in 1916, and German East Africa under the command of Von Lettow surrendered in 1918. With the end of the Great War, the German Colonial Empire ceased to exist, and all of its former colonies were partitioned and split between the Allied powers. With the emergence of the Third Reich and the start of the Second World War, the Germans created new plans for regaining territories in Africa, which they never managed to implement successfully.

Chapter 6: Lessons for Today

Although the Great War is remembered largely for its staggering human cost, the brutal attrition warfare in the trenches, and its profound geopolitical repercussions, at its core lies a catastrophic failure of diplomacy. The inability of the European powers to resolve disputes through negotiation set the stage for a devastating global conflict that they could have easily avoided. Their diplomatic missteps that sparked and prolonged the war remain strikingly relevant in the modern world, offering crucial lessons about alliance-building, miscommunication, and the unintended consequences of political maneuvering. Understanding their failures sheds light on contemporary international relations, where echoes of World War I-era diplomacy continue to influence global policies and conflicts. Naturally, this leads us to ask: What can we learn from this today?

There is no doubt that one of the most crucial diplomatic errors that eventually led to the Great War was the overly independent and rigid system of alliances. By the time the 20th century arrived,

Europe had separated into two major "blocs": the Triple Alliance, comprising Austria-Hungary, Italy, and Germany; and the Triple Entente, composed of Russia, France, and Britain. These alliances, meant to deter conflict through mutual defense agreements, ultimately had the opposite effect. When tensions escalated in 1914, they were snares that transformed what should have been a regional conflict between Austria-Hungary and Serbia into a world war.

Modern parallels, such as today's NATO and other regional defense agreements like ANZUS and ASEAN, are strikingly similar. And even though these alliances offer security, they also risk escalating minor conflicts into larger ones. Sadly, today we are seeing minor conflicts springing up everywhere. Places like the Balkans, the Middle East, Palestine, and Ukraine are experiencing conflict that could quickly spiral out of control. The diplomatic failures of the Great War show that rigid alliances can limit flexibility and lead nations into avoidable confrontation.

Another fundamental factor contributing to the outbreak of the Great War was nationalism. Alongside militarism, it played a crucial role in undermining diplomatic efforts in the years leading up to World War I. Sweeping nationalist fervor —

especially among the Slavic populations in the Balkans — resulted in aggressive posturing and a willingness to risk all-out war in pursuit of national and ethnic prestige. When Archduke Franz Ferdinand was assassinated by a Slavic Serb nationalist, Austria-Hungary's response was quite harsh. It was driven by a lasting desire to "come out on top," to preserve its prestige, and reassert its dominance over the subjugated Slavs and their nationalist movements. All the while, Germany's "place in the sun" rhetoric (i.e., its imperialist foreign policy that stated *"We wish to throw no one into the shade, but we also demand our own place in the sun"*) justified the rapid militarization of the entire nation. Thus, Germanic and Slavic nationalism came into direct confrontation, perhaps as a culmination of centuries of inter-ethnic strife.

WORLD WAR 1

American cartoon showing territorial dispute between France and Germany over Alsace-Lorraine, 1898.

In the years leading up to the war, nationalism was more than a political stance: it was an ideology that permeated every facet of society. Newspapers, literature, and public speeches glorified national superiority, fostering a culture where compromise was equated with weakness. Governments increasingly leaned on nationalist sentiment to rally public support, which in turn emboldened more aggressive foreign policy. Leaders found themselves in a precarious position in which diplomatic concessions were seen as betrayals, rendering peaceful negotiation politically untenable.

WORLD WAR 1

One would think that the threat posed by nationalism would have been understood, exposed, and dispensed with after the calamitous Great War, but it was not to be. Just twenty years later, Germany would be swept up in a whirlwind of nationalism, one that would lead it into the Second World War, which was even more vicious and horrifying than the one preceding it. What we have seen over time is a moderation of nationalism in some regions. Unfortunately, it continues to exert its influence across much of the world.

Furthermore, nationalism's far-reaching influence was instrumental in contributing to the war's duration and intensity. All the involved nations upheld their beliefs in their own moral and military superiority, and this led to their refusal to seek early peace settlements, so as not to mar their sense of superiority. Not even the mounting casualties, the countless dead and maimed, or the economic hardships would alter their opinions. This is because, ultimately, governments feared losing face in front of their nationalist-minded populations. And it was this stubborn persistence that prolonged the war far beyond what the belligerents' military leaders had initially anticipated.

But what about today? How does nationalism appear in the modern age? Although not as "crude" as it was in the years of the Great War, nationalism is prevalent in several countries and remains a considerable factor in global politics. Nationalism remains strong in China, Russia, and North Korea, while there are rising nationalist sentiments evident in the U.S. It's a trend that has led to trade wars, arms races, and strained diplomatic relations. Brexit, the rise of far-right and populist movements across Europe, and protectionist economic policies all reflect a resurgence of nationalism reminiscent of the early 20th century. The lesson from World War I is clear: nationalism, if left unchecked, can make diplomatic resolutions impossible, as it prioritizes national pride over pragmatic negotiation. Just as in 1914, modern nationalism fosters an "us versus them" mentality, which can transform regional disputes into global conflicts.

Perhaps the most striking of all the failures of World War I diplomacy was the sheer prevalence of miscommunication and misunderstanding among European leaders. Germany wrongly believed that Britain would remain neutral if a war erupted, while Austria-Hungary believed that Russia would not intervene in a conflict with Serbia. Both were completely wrong. There is no doubt that their miscalculations were based on incomplete diplomatic exchanges and a lack of clear signaling. After all, diplomatic channels before the Great War were often slow, inconsistent, and frequently misinterpreted. Foreign ministers and ambassadors sometimes acted on misleading and outdated information, leading to contradictory messages exchanged between allies. Notably, the July Crisis of 1914 was marked by utter confusion. Austria-Hungary delayed delivering its ultimatum to Serbia, Russia hesitated with its mobilization, and Germany's "blank cheque" (i.e., a situation in which an agreement has been made that is open-ended or vague) of promised support to Austria-Hungary was grossly misinterpreted as a call for immediate war.

And even within governments, leaders failed to coordinate clear responses. Kaiser Wilhelm II issued conflicting directives regarding war preparation, while Britain's government was divided on whether to intervene. These failures in communication made diplomacy nearly impossible at the most critical moment in European history.

Even in the modern era, diplomatic miscommunication remains a persistent threat to global stability. The Cuban Missile Crisis, the 2003 Iraq War, and recent tensions between the United States and China over Taiwan show how misinterpreting intentions can escalate matters.

Unlike 1914, however, the presence of nuclear weapons makes the consequences of diplomatic miscalculations today even more severe. The lessons from the Great War highlight the need for clearer diplomatic messaging, real-time intelligence-sharing, and open channels of communication to prevent unnecessary escalations into military action.

Even after the war ended, diplomatic failures continued to shape global conflicts. The Treaty of Versailles in 1919 imposed punitive reparations on Germany, fostering resentment that contributed to the eventual rise of Adolf Hitler and the Second World War. Rather than stabilizing Europe, the treaty sowed the seeds of future conflict by humiliating Germany and forcing it into economic turmoil. The treaty's terms included territorial losses, military restrictions, and a significant debt burden, which influenced Germany's future actions. The League of Nations, created in response to the war's devastation, proved ineffective in preventing future conflicts. It lacked enforcement mechanisms, and key powers like the United States refused to join, weakening its ability to act as a global peacekeeper. The failure of post-World War I diplomacy highlights the necessity of ensuring that peace agreements are both just and enforceable. Rather than focusing on punishment, diplomatic efforts should aim at stability and long-term cooperation.

Even today, these hard-learned lessons remain highly relevant, particularly in the realm of post-war diplomacy. The aftermath of conflicts in Iraq, Afghanistan, and Syria has demonstrated that poorly designed peace settlements often lead to prolonged instability. The diplomatic failures post-World War I serve as a reminder that lasting peace requires fair and enforceable agreements, not punitive measures that breed future resentment.

Ultimately, the profound diplomatic failures that occurred in the Great War provide important lessons for contemporary international relations and cannot be overlooked. The obvious dangers of rigid alliances, unchecked nationalism, diplomatic miscommunication, punitive peace settlements, economic rivalries, and propaganda continue to shape global politics. In an era of increasing geopolitical tension, learning from the past is more crucial than ever. The world today stands at a crossroads much like 1914, and the choices made by global leaders will determine whether history repeats itself or if diplomacy can finally succeed where it once failed.

It is important to remember that the Great War was fought not only on the battlefields of Europe, in the trenches, the skies, and the fields. It was fought just as fiercely in the minds of civilians and soldiers. On both sides of the conflict, governments understood the immense power of information (and misinformation as well), recognizing it as a potent weapon. As a result, propaganda was employed on a never-before-seen scale, shaping the mindsets of many, both before and during the war. In fact, it was the first global conflict in which propaganda played a central role. As governments sought to rally major support for the war, control the narrative, maintain national morale, and demonize the enemy, propaganda became a major tool for them to achieve their goals. It was disseminated through various media, including newspapers, posters, films, speeches, and even literature. Its primary goal was recruiting and mobilizing soldiers to maintain the war effort. Thus, recruitment campaigns became an aggressive hotbed of propaganda use. In Britain, the famous "Your Country Needs You" propaganda poster, featuring the British Secretary of State for War, Lord Kitchener, became an emblematic symbol of patriotic duty, and Britons enlisted en masse.

WORLD WAR 1

British propaganda posters from the Great War.

Similarly, in the United States, posters of Uncle Sam pointing directly at the viewer and declaring "*I Want You for U.S. Army*" became iconic. Propaganda campaigns often framed enlistment as a matter of national honor and masculine responsibility. In Germany and France, conscription was supplemented with posters depicting enemy aggression, urging men to protect their homelands. Women were also targeted by propaganda imploring them to encourage their male relatives to enlist, with messages implying that true patriots would not hesitate to fight. Mobilization efforts extended far beyond the battlefield, as propaganda urged civilians to support the war through industrial labor, increased food production, and the purchase of war bonds. Central to this effort was the demonization of the enemy — one of the most powerful and pervasive tools of wartime propaganda. Governments would portray the enemy nations, leaders, and soldiers as inhumane and monstrous, further fueling nationalistic fervor and justifying the brutal conduct of war on the front lines. For example, the British press widely circulated stories of German atrocities in Belgium, creating a new form of "atrocity propaganda." They exaggerated or fabricated stories of soldiers committing mass executions and mutilations, such as the infamous

WORLD WAR 1

"Rape of Belgium" narrative, which, although based on real events, was greatly amplified to present the Germans (derogatorily called the "Huns"), as cruel, barbaric oppressors. In return, the Germans depicted the British and the French in a somewhat less exaggerated but more realistic light: the former were depicted as selfish and ruthless imperialists and colonizers, and the latter as weak and decadent. The United States didn't lag behind either. After joining the Great War in 1917, they immediately launched an aggressive anti-German propaganda campaign, popularizing the popular term "Hun" — an allusion to the savagery of nomadic invaders in history, particularly the Huns under Attila. Cartoons and posters depicted German soldiers as bloodthirsty brutes preying on innocent civilians, further entrenching a sense of moral superiority among the Allies. Such demonization played a crucial role in maintaining public support for the war and dehumanizing the enemy, making violence against them more palatable.

Governments similarly relied on civilians to contribute to the war effort by conserving resources, purchasing war bonds, and working in munitions factories. In the United States, slogans like *"Food Will Win the War"* promoted rationing and boosted agricultural production. Posters and pamphlets reinforced the idea that every civilian played a role in securing victory. Women were particularly targeted, urged to take on factory work, join auxiliary military services, or manage household resources efficiently to aid the war effort. In Britain, the government launched the "Women's Land Army" campaign, encouraging women to take over agricultural roles vacated by the men who had gone to war. The war also spurred industrial innovations, as nations had to rapidly expand their production of arms, ammunition, and other wartime supplies. Propaganda linked industrial labor to patriotism, portraying factory workers as essential to victory. War bonds were another major component of economic propaganda. Posters prodded citizens to invest in the war, framing it as both a civic duty and a financially sound decision. Countries like the United States used celebrity endorsements and mass rallies to encourage participation in these financial initiatives.

Despite these efforts, as the war dragged on, maintaining public confidence became increasingly difficult. Governments took a one-sided approach to maintaining morale, suppressing defeatist views and news, downplaying setbacks, and highlighting victories, even if they were minor. The media played a major role in this effort, often portraying an overly optimistic picture of the war to bolster public support. Soldiers at the front were depicted as unwavering heroes, and battlefield setbacks were downplayed or omitted from the narrative entirely. Propaganda also sought to instill a sense of resilience among civilians, encouraging them to endure hardships for the greater good, such as rationing and losing loved ones. In Germany, slogans like *"Durchhalten!"* ("Hold out!") were used to maintain morale despite severe food shortages and economic hardship. In Britain and France, propaganda emphasized national unity and sacrifice, portraying the war as a battle for civilization itself. Poetry, music, and literature also played a role in boosting spirits, with patriotic songs and uplifting poems reinforcing a sense of duty and hope. In the trenches, newspapers and entertainment troupes helped maintain soldiers' spirits, offering humor and distraction from the horrors of war. The sustained use of propaganda to maintain morale was essential in preventing war fatigue from undermining the national effort.

One effective method for disseminating information to civilians was through the use of detailed and elaborately painted posters. They were often quite visually striking and fairly easy to disseminate. They featured emotionally charged imagery, catchy patriotic slogans, and dramatic appeals to sacrifice, duty, work, and national pride. All the nations involved in the Great War worked tirelessly to produce thousands of these posters in an attempt to persuade the populace to fight and support the war effort.

The psychology behind this was quite simple: visual imagery works in evoking strong emotional responses. Through the cunning use of striking colors, bold typography, and dramatic, lifelike compositions, propaganda posters captured people's attention quickly and made strong impressions on them. For example, recruitment posters usually depicted heroic soldiers, standing defiantly against the enemy, protecting innocents, or fiercely charging into battle. Other themes included mothers and children, the duty of men toward their families, and workers hard-pressed in their jobs. Additionally, the use of symbolism was common. Images of lions, eagles, other "noble" animals, and national flags emphasized themes of nobility, elitism, strength, and unity.

Perhaps the most despicable aspect of these posters was their deliberate use of fear and guilt to compel people to take action. By depicting gruesome scenes of death and destruction allegedly caused by the enemy, propaganda posters aimed to compel citizens to enlist and support the war effort. They suggested that only a citizen's involvement could prevent war's horrors from reaching their own lives and homes. Besides this, women were also a constantly used subject, depicted as either vulnerable figures in need of protection, or as strong and determined workers aiding the war economy. The effectiveness of these visuals lay in their ability to communicate complex messages instantly, ensuring that even those who were illiterate could grasp their meaning. And so, the posters targeted both men and women, both young and old, ensuring that every citizen would — in one way or another — become involved in the war effort.

Newspapers were equally vital, as they were a formidable medium for disseminating propaganda, as they could do so on a massive scale. Read by all segments of society, they became the primary tool for shaping public perception and thought during the war. As a result, governments took extensive measures to control the information presented to the general public. For example, the British government established the War Propaganda Bureau (Wellington House), which worked closely with newspapers to ensure that only favorable reports would reach the general public. Journalists were strictly prohibited from reporting directly from the front lines, and information was heavily censored to prevent negative coverage that could lower the populace's morale. The Defense of the Realm Act (DORA), passed in Britain in 1914, allowed the government to suppress any publication deemed harmful to the war effort. Consequently, reports of casualties and defeats were downplayed, while in stark contrast, the victories (no matter how minor) made the headlines and were prominently covered. In Germany as well, the newspapers were strictly monitored by the military, and journalists who published critical content faced imprisonment. The United States followed a similar path after entering the war in 1917, enacting the Espionage Act, which criminalized criticism of the government's war policies.

But despite government censorship, underground and independent publications sometimes managed to provide alternative perspectives. Some soldiers kept secret diaries detailing the grim realities of trench warfare, and in the latter stages of the war, growing public skepticism led to increased questioning of official reports. Nevertheless, for much of the war, government-controlled newspapers played an essential role in maintaining support for the war effort.

Chapter 7:
The Horrors of Trench Warfare

The Great War featured numerous technological innovations and advancements that transformed the nature of warfare. However, there was one aspect that set it apart from all other conflicts: trench warfare. Closely linked to the emerging strategy of attrition warfare, it was characterized by sieges, stalemates, and grueling battles designed to grind down the enemy over time. Trench warfare was a direct result of a newly emerging mode of conflict, in which new tactics, weapons, and increased firepower reigned over the traditional infantry soldier. This created an environment where a successful defender was at an advantage. So, in order to gain the upper hand, combatants relied on elaborate and extensive networks of trenches and dugouts. These complex trench networks were utilized mostly along the Western Front. Trench warfare resulted in severe casualties for any side that attempted to cross the "no man's land" in between trench systems during offensive operations, which clearly indicated that the defender had the advantage.

WORLD WAR 1

During and after the Great War, trench warfare came to symbolize the horror, senselessness,, and staggering loss of life in the conflict, as well as the devastating nature of a global war of attrition. Coordinated trench attacks were marked by futile charges and extremely high casualties, making them a powerful emblem of war's futility. In the Great War, "going over the top" was synonymous with certain death: in all the great battles of the Western Front, tens of thousands of young men would lose their lives without even firing a single shot or making any contribution whatsoever to their side. They were simply mowed down by machine guns and artillery before they could even reach the enemy trenches. It was a disastrous shift in military doctrine. Enemy machine gunners, sharpshooters, and riflemen all had a clear shot at the advancing soldiers. A stark example of the carnage caused by mass infantry charges is the first day of the Battle of the Somme in 1916. In less than 24 hours, the British lost 60,000 young men, gaining little in return.

The Great War was certainly a cruel testing ground of enormous scale. Each year saw new tactics and technologies from one side that the other side was forced to adapt to. In the first years of the war, trenches were seen by both sides as a reliable method of defense.

WORLD WAR 1

A good trench system was designed as an almost continuous and complex network. It had a large number of connections between parallel trenches, making for an efficient system of communications and resupply. Depending on their depth and complexity, trenches were meant to be a very efficient defense against the constant threat of artillery. As soldiers were underground while they were in a trench, they were better shielded than if they were in concrete structures above-ground, and were protected from everything but a direct hit. Trenches were considered a reliable approach to warfare simply because of the ubiquitous use of artillery during the Great War.

WORLD WAR 1

German soldiers in a trench, 1916

Of course, it is important to consider the time during which the Great War was fought. As the

WORLD WAR 1

20th century marched forward, the grand, set-piece battles that had once been common practice quickly became a thing of the past. The glory days of Napoleon and his contemporaries were long gone; now was the era of attrition, industry, and widespread destruction. The strategies of the Napoleonic era no longer held the key to victory. This time, it was all about devastation — heavy bombardment and continuous grinding were what would break the enemy. From the days of cavalry charges and rigid battle lines, soldiers were thrust into the dirt and mud of trench warfare, where the fighting became a test of endurance and nerve, and only the toughest could hope to survive the grinding chaos of attrition.

Trenches came in a few different designs, which mostly depended on their function and strategic position. Those of greater significance had to have a complex and sturdy design that also provided adequate living conditions for the soldiers who had to live in them. This meant that a quality trench had a depth of at least 8 feet (approximately 2.5 meters), so men could stand upright without being in the line of fire. What is more, the best trench systems were almost never simply straight; instead, they relied on a tactical zig-zag or step pattern, where each straight section was just a few feet long. This design had a distinct advantage, as it limited the effects of artillery shells or grenades that exploded within the trench, since the stepped design contained much of the blast. Similarly, it was also an efficient way to remove the threat of enfilade fire if the trench was assaulted. (Enfilade refers to gunfire directed in a straight line, along the length of an enemy formation — it was a very real threat in straight-line trenches.)

The better trenches had further advantageous features, such as bottoms lined with wood ("duckboards") or raised wooden frames. They gave the soldiers' footwear a firmer grip while moving through the trenches, while keeping rainwater and mud below and off their boots. The side walls of the trench would be lined with materials such as boards, corrugated iron sheets, and sandbags. Of course, throughout the war, trenches varied according to their owners and location. The French and British trenches typically adhered to established construction techniques and dimensions, while the Germans sometimes employed different methods. Their trenches were a bit deeper — usually around 4 meters (12 feet) — and often included specialized dugouts for officers, storage and sleeping quarters, as well as tunnels that extended several stories underground.

WORLD WAR 1

It goes without saying that trench warfare brought an entirely new aspect to a soldier's life, a life that now required adaptation, perseverance, fear, and sacrifice. A soldier could spend as long as two weeks in a forward, frontline trench, or as little as a single day, before being relieved and sent elsewhere. That meant a trench system needed to allow for some humane conditions as much as possible. The time spent in a trench varied according to nationality and available manpower.

But even with high-quality construction, life in the trenches was almost never humane and livable. For a good portion of the year, life in the trenches was hampered by constant mud, water, dampness, and disease. Even with the tactical advantages of a trench defense system, death rates were still high, mainly due to the almost incessant artillery fire. An incredible 75% of all known casualties in the trenches can be attributed to artillery fire. The men who were not the recipients of a direct hit would frequently succumb to the resulting shrapnel's devastating effects.

WORLD WAR 1

Trenches of the 11th Cheshire Regiment at Ovillers-la-Boisselle, on the Somme, July 1916.

Another major cause of death in the trenches was disease from poor hygiene. The most common illness was trench fever, which was spread by body lice — a constant nuisance for soldiers. While typically a non-fatal illness, trench fever was often deadly during the Great War due to limited medical knowledge and the harsh conditions at the front lines. It caused nausea, rashes, fever, and continual lethargy. Furthermore, poor conditions meant that in a trench, any minor infection could be fatal. Wounds were often left untreated, and they would fester and frequently become fatal. Add to this the inability to properly dispose of the mass of casualties, and one is left with a truly grim and unforgiving image — just another of the Great War's numerous, ugly characteristics. Trench warfare also brought a different approach to combat. Soldiers had to constantly adapt to new conditions and devise new and inventive ways to defeat their enemy and gain an upper hand in the trenches' cramped and unforgiving conditions. First and foremost among improvisations was the grenade. Its worth was quickly noticed, so much so that hand grenades became a preferred weapon of most soldiers. Properly thrown, a grenade could have devastating effects in a narrow trench. Not only would the blast kill or wound several soldiers, but the grenade could be used without exposing the attacker to enemy fire. What followed was the development of unique methods of increasing the distance a grenade could be thrown. Rifle-mounted rods for grenade launching, crossbow-type launchers, and the iconic German "potato masher" were typical examples of the era's ingenious designs.

But when it came to hand-to-hand combat (the most frightening part of trench warfare), grenades and rifles often came in second place. If a group of soldiers managed to cross no man's land and invade an enemy trench, fierce close-quarter combat typically followed. In a trench's tight spaces, bolt-action rifles were difficult to use effectively, and throwing a grenade risked harming nearby comrades. Therefore, soldiers relied on a very primitive aspect of warfare, borrowing designs from medieval periods. There were all sorts of new melee weapons, the most common of which was the trench club. Typically, it was a crude bludgeon made by company smiths and engineers from whatever parts could be scrounged. Trench clubs were brutal and highly effective in hand-to-hand combat, and were widely used during the Great War, thanks to their efficiency. Specially designed knives were also used. While bayonets were standard issue and designed for close combat, many soldiers didn't like them because they proved to be unwieldy and prone to getting stuck in a pierced enemy. This gave rise to combat trench knives and brass knuckles, with which one could kill an enemy swiftly and efficiently and continue fighting almost immediately afterward.

Still, in order to use these medieval melee weapons, soldiers first needed to successfully cross no man's land. And that was a daunting challenge in and of itself. In crossing no man's land, a soldier would need to deal with one of the most menacing and troublesome barriers a man could face: barbed wire. It was a barrier that was simple in its design, but extremely effective at stopping advancing enemy infantry. It was the direct cause of untold numbers of casualties on both sides. Also known as razor wire, it would be placed all along the front line and would be very difficult to bypass once it was secured in place. A soldier who faced this obstacle was forced to either cut through it, find an opening, or bypass it in some other way. Failing to do so could result in a quick death: a man could quickly get stuck in the jumble of wires, which would expose him to enemy fire and make him an easy target. If he managed to free himself, he would end up with several cuts, which could get infected soon after and ultimately prove fatal. Frequently, barbed wire was positioned so it would be within the field of fire of defending machine guns, which would inflict heavy losses on trapped soldiers.

There is little doubt that trench warfare was one of the ugliest and cruelest aspects of the Great War. It was a nightmarish depiction of how wartime battlefield conditions can quickly degrade to become inhuman when the war becomes static and enters the attrition phase. From the Somme to Ypres and Passchendaele, and all the way to the hilly Dolomites and the Eastern Front, trenches were the inescapable part of this deadly conflict. With history as a silent witness, we can say with certainty that no one would have wanted to be in that muddy hell, where each passing minute brought a new expectation of a truly grim and frightening end, and death lurked around every corner. Trench warfare meant only one thing was certain for the common soldier of the First World War: fear.

Chapter 8: The Last Thunderclap

By the autumn of 1917, the First World War had entered a phase of accelerated exhaustion. Any hope that one offensive could bring a decisive breakthrough had long since been lost in the mud of Flanders and the snows of the Eastern Front. What remained was a war of attrition so grinding and relentless that even the victors would emerge from it battered and irrevocably changed. The turning point for the Central Powers began not on the Western Front, but in the East. Russia's withdrawal from the war in the wake of the Bolshevik Revolution in 1917 seemed at first a windfall for Germany, a moment of respite. The Treaty of Brest-Litovsk, signed in March 1918, officially ended hostilities between the Russian Soviet Federative Socialist Republic and the Central Powers. It allowed Germany to redirect over fifty divisions to the Western Front, finally giving the German High Command the manpower it needed to attempt a knockout blow against Britain and France before American forces arrived in full strength. Yet, while Germany had won peace in the East, it had not won stability. The occupation of vast swaths of Eastern Europe overextended

Germany's resources, and the promised spoils of victory never materialized. On top of that, the ideological virus of revolution that had infected Russia now began to fester within the German state itself.

Despite increasing internal weakness, Germany launched its last great gamble in March 1918: the Spring Offensive, or *Kaiserschlacht* ("Kaiser's Battle"). Under General Erich Ludendorff's command, the German army launched a series of attacks aimed at breaking the Allied lines before American forces could tilt the balance. Operation Michael, the first of several offensives, achieved dramatic initial success. Utilizing stormtrooper tactics and infiltration units, German forces broke through British positions on the Somme, advanced rapidly, and came perilously close to capturing Amiens, an essential logistical hub. The offensive, however, lacked strategic coherence. Tactical victories were not reinforced by clear objectives, and German troops advanced into a vacuum, without sufficient supply lines or reserves. By July, Ludendorff's offensives had culminated in over 1 million casualties, territorial gains that could not be held, and an exhausted army that had expended its final reserves of men and morale.

WORLD WAR 1

Meanwhile, the Allied powers, now under the unified command of French General Ferdinand Foch, began to regain the initiative. The arrival of American forces in significant numbers in 1918 bolstered Allied strength at a critical moment. Though initially inexperienced, American troops under General John J. Pershing brought renewed energy and a numerical advantage. Their participation in the Second Battle of the Marne in July 1918 marked a key moment in turning the tide. The German offensive was not only repelled, but was also followed by a devastating counterattack. For the first time, it became clear to German commanders that the initiative had passed irreversibly to the Allies. From this point onward, the German army was on the defensive.

The Allied counteroffensive, known as the Hundred Days Offensive, began in August 1918 and continued until the Armistice in November. Unlike earlier, static campaigns, this was a mobile, relentless push involving coordinated artillery, tanks, infantry, and air support. The Battle of Amiens on August 8th was dubbed *"the black day of the German Army"* by Ludendorff himself. The German lines buckled under the weight of the assault. The Allies used deception, creeping barrages, and air superiority to sow confusion and disrupt the Germans' ability to coordinate their defenses. The battles of Saint-Mihiel and Meuse-Argonne saw massive American involvement, while British and Dominion forces — including Australians and Canadians — proved instrumental in cracking the Hindenburg Line, a supposedly impregnable series of German fortifications. The German retreat was now a rout, compounded by mass surrenders and mounting desertions.

A destroyed German trench on the Western Front.

Even as the front lines collapsed, the home front was disintegrating even faster. In Germany and Austria-Hungary, economic starvation, political unrest, and the psychological burden of endless war brought national life to a breaking point. In October 1918, Germany was plagued by strikes, mutinies, and the first stirrings of revolution. The Kiel Mutiny, which began with sailors refusing a suicidal last sortie, quickly spread throughout the country. Workers' and soldiers' councils, inspired by the Soviet model, formed spontaneously in cities. Kaiser Wilhelm II, increasingly isolated and powerless, abdicated on November 9th, 1918, fleeing to the Netherlands. The German Empire, which had been founded in 1871 in the Hall of Mirrors at Versailles, collapsed within days into a republic declared in Berlin's streets. The Austro-Hungarian Empire fared no better. Long a patchwork of ethnicities that could barely be held together, the dual monarchy unraveled as national movements seized their moment. The Czechs, Slovaks, Slovenes, Croats, Serbs, Poles, and others declared independence or aligned with the victorious Allies. Emperor Karl I, having lost control over his army and his territories, announced he would relinquish participation in state affairs on November 11, though he refused to formally abdicate. The Habsburg monarchy, which had ruled Central Europe for centuries, ceased to exist. In the Balkans, chaos reigned as the territorial ambitions of emerging nation-states like Serbia and Romania collided with imperial collapse, setting the stage for future instability.

WORLD WAR 1

The Ottoman Empire, too, succumbed in the final months of the war. Defeated in the Middle East by the British (often aided by Arab revolts inspired by promises of post-war independence), the Ottomans signed the Armistice of Mudros on October 30th, 1918. The once-vast Islamic empire, already hollowed out by decades of decline, was carved up by the victorious Western powers in the postwar settlements. Its final dissolution would come in the aftermath of the war, during the Turkish War of Independence and the abolition of the sultanate in 1922.

On November 11th, 1918, at 11:00 a.m., the guns finally fell silent. The armistice signed in a railway carriage in Compiègne ended the fighting, though not the suffering. Europe had been bled dry. Over 9 million soldiers and at least 7 million civilians had perished. The war left legions of wounded soldiers, who were scarred both physically and psychologically. Entire regions lay in ruin, and an influenza epidemic, exacerbated by conditions brought about by the war, claimed tens of millions more lives. The end of the fighting did not mean the arrival of peace. The Paris Peace Conference, which opened in January 1919, proved a venue for recrimination as much as reconstruction. The Treaty of Versailles, signed in June 1919, imposed severe territorial losses, military restrictions, and reparations on Germany. Its infamous Article 231, the "war guilt clause," placed sole responsibility for the war on Germany's shoulders — a humiliation that would echo bitterly through the decades to come. Similarly, the redrawing of borders across Eastern Europe and the Middle East sowed seeds of future conflict. Ethnic minorities found themselves trapped in newly created states, while colonial subjects who had fought for the Allies received neither recognition nor independence.

WORLD WAR 1

The railway carriage in which the armistice was signed.

In the United States, the war's end brought a return to isolationism. Though President Woodrow Wilson had championed the League of Nations as a mechanism to prevent future wars, the U.S. Senate refused to ratify the Versailles treaty or join the organization. Without American involvement, the League would lack the authority and influence to enforce peace, a flaw that would become tragically clear in the 1930s.

The war's cultural legacy was profound. The optimism of the prewar era gave way to disillusionment and cynicism. The "Lost Generation" of artists, writers, and thinkers grappled with the trauma of industrialized death and the breakdown of old certainties. In Germany, economic hardship and national humiliation festered into resentment, fueling the rise of extremist ideologies. The world had changed irrevocably. Modern warfare had shown itself to be all-encompassing, indiscriminate, and mechanized. No longer could war be romanticized as a noble endeavor. It was now understood for what it was: a devastating crucible of modernity's darkest impulses.

The late stages of World War I were marked by chaos, desperation, and collapse, but also by transformation. Empires died, nations were born, and the very concept of war was redefined.

And so, the war ended, not with triumph, but with exhaustion. It left behind not victors and vanquished, but a wounded world groping for meaning in the aftermath. The road to peace would be long and troubled, and in less than two decades, the world would once again descend into darkness. But in the final quiet of November 11th, 1918, there was, at least for a moment, silence, and the fragile hope that the storm had passed.

Chapter 9:
How People Rebuilt After the War

The end of the Great War in November 1918 marked the close of one of the most devastating conflicts in human history. Yet, it signaled a new beginning, a long and arduous process of rebuilding and starting anew. World War I ravaged entire nations, reduced cities and towns to rubble, displaced hundreds of thousands, and left millions of dead. Economies lay in ruins, governments had collapsed, and the psychological scars of the "War to End All Wars" ran terribly deep. But amid this apocalyptic destruction, there rang out a unified call for continuation. People across the globe had to survive, rebuild, and move forward. In the decades that followed, they worked tirelessly to build new homes, economies, and societies, forging new political landscapes and establishing institutions aimed at preventing future catastrophes.

It goes without saying that the physical destruction brought about by the Great War was immense. The

Western Front, which had stretched from Belgium to France, had seen entire cities and towns reduced to rubble and effectively wiped from existence. During the four years of obliterating warfare, the economic centers of France — Reims, Arras, and Ypres — were utterly devastated. The same was true for major railway hubs and industrial regions, which suffered equally severe damage. And so, the priority lay in rebuilding the infrastructure in this part of Europe, especially Belgium and France, where much of the fighting took place.

Georges Clemenceau took up the reins of the French government and enacted large-scale reconstruction programs to restore industries, transportation networks, and housing. These reconstruction efforts were partially funded through German reparations, but payments were inconsistent and often politically contentious. And thus, France adopted a unique "pay-as-you-go" model, which meant that they had to rebuild as funds became available. The French relied on both private investments and state-led initiatives aimed at revitalizing rural areas and major urban centers.

Belgium likewise met similarly enormous rebuilding challenges, especially in Flanders. This region's fertile farmland, picturesque fields, and small hamlets had been turned into a true hellish wasteland due to constant bombardment and massive trench networks. Belgian efforts mainly focused on reconstructing essential infrastructure and reviving agriculture, often with assistance from foreign investors and aid organizations. In defeated Germany, war-torn regions were slowly rebuilt with the limited resources at hand, as the nation struggled with major economic instability and the rigid constraints imposed on it by the Treaty of Versailles, which limited its capability to effectively mobilize any significant resources.

Elsewhere, in Eastern Europe, scars also ran deep. This region had endured intense fighting, repeated invasions, and rapidly shifting front lines. Scarred and restless, Eastern Europe faced the formidable challenge of rebuilding. Poland, newly reconstituted as an independent state, had to rebuild its cities and infrastructure while simultaneously establishing its government. The country faced significant logistical and economic challenges, particularly since it had been divided among three empires (Russian, German, and Austro-Hungarian) before the war. What is more, entirely new nations were emerging in the area in the aftermath of the ravaging war. These were Czechoslovakia and Yugoslavia, two newly formed independent Slavic nations whose people had finally rid themselves of the oppressive Austro-

Hungarian yoke and so faced an entirely new beginning. For them, it was equally as hard as for the larger nations, as they dealt with limited national budgets and the many difficulties entailed in a fresh start.

Ruins of Ypres, 1919

It goes without saying that the First World War placed exorbitant financial burdens on all the nations involved. After all, war is a costly endeavor. For most of them, the war's cost had been astronomical, and in its aftermath, national economies were in shambles. Britain and France emerged from the war heavily indebted to the United States, while Germany, already debilitated by its defeat, faced the additional challenge of paying the reparations dictated by the Treaty of Versailles.

In Britain, the 1925 return to the gold standard was meant to restore financial stability. However, it ultimately contributed to deflation and economic stagnation. Additionally, the war ended up leaving Britain reliant on its vast empire for further economic resources, which in turn led to heightened tensions in its colonial holdings and a resultant weakening of Britain's "imperial" strength. France, facing major inflation and economic stagnation, implemented policies to encourage industrial growth and foreign investment. The French devalued the franc in 1928 to stabilize the economy and implemented protectionist measures to shield their domestic industries.

Unsurprisingly, Germany's economy suffered even more after the war. The Weimar Republic (the German state that had emerged post-war) had major struggles with hyperinflation in the early 1920s, as the value of the German mark collapsed to catastrophically low levels. The economic crisis necessitated foreign intervention, leading to the Dawes Plan of 1924, which restructured Germany's reparations payments and facilitated loans from the United States to stabilize Germany's economy. This temporary economic relief allowed for some recovery, but Germany remained vulnerable to external shocks, as would be seen with the Great Depression in 1929.

In stark contrast, the United States emerged as the foremost global economic power, and it played a crucial role in the overall postwar recovery. American banks and businesses invested in European reconstruction, and the U.S. provided economic assistance through loans and trade agreements. However, this financial interconnectedness made global economies vulnerable to future downturns, which would be demonstrated in the Great Depression.

But the war did not simply reshape national borders; it also transformed political landscapes. Several empires collapsed as a result of the Great War, namely the Ottoman, Russian, German, and Austro-Hungarian Empires. The fall of these giants created a vast power vacuum, ushering in a wave of new changes across post-war Europe. Newly established nations and revolutionary movements emerged, shaping the future as we know it today. In 1917, the Russian revolution of the Bolsheviks set the stage for the swift rise of the Soviet Union, while in Central Europe, the newly formed nations of Poland, Yugoslavia, and Czechoslovakia sought to establish stable governments. This was not so easy, not amid rising ethnic tensions in the Balkans and many economic challenges.

WORLD WAR 1

In Western Europe, the war further reinforced democratic governance in France and Britain, yet it also sowed the seeds of political instability. Italy, despite ending on the winning side, faced widespread economic difficulties and social unrest. It experienced a tumultuous period that paved the way for the rise of Benito Mussolini and the ascension of fascism in 1922. The Weimar Republic struggled to maintain stability, as both the left and the right sides of the political spectrum descended into political extremism. Germany's political situation, coupled with its economic crisis, allowed the rise of the National Socialist party and its leader, Adolf Hitler. Given all this, we can see that the Great War was not the "war to end all wars," but instead was a grim introduction to an age of warfare that would prove to be even darker and more horrifying.

Socially, the war had accelerated changes in gender roles and labor dynamics. Women, having played a crucial role in wartime industries and services, sought greater rights and recognition. In Britain, women over 30 were granted the right to vote in 1918, followed by universal suffrage in 1928. Similar movements gained momentum in France, Germany, and the United States, with women's suffrage being enacted in many countries during the interwar period.

WORLD WAR 1

Beyond the immense economic and physical devastation caused by the war were the deep psychological scars it left on those who survived. Hundreds of thousands of returning soldiers suffered from what was then called "shell shock" — a condition we now recognize as PTSD. These men often struggled to reintegrate into civilian life, having been so severely affected by the constant violence and stress they experienced on the front lines. They now faced unemployment, emotional trauma, physical disabilities, and strained relationships. Governments and medical institutions established major rehabilitation programs, but treatment for their severe psychological scarring remained inadequate. After all they went through, these men deserved better, but better never came.

However, at the same time, societies sought adequate ways to memorialize their fallen and make their sacrifices known and remembered. All over Europe, war memorials were erected in towns and cities, meant to honor those poor souls who perished in the war. In Britain, the Cenotaph in London and the Tomb of the Unknown Warrior in Westminster Abbey became national symbols of mourning. France built the Ossuary at Douaumont to commemorate the fallen at Verdun, while Germany, despite economic hardships, constructed war cemeteries and monuments to remember its dead. The United States, which had entered the war later, also erected memorials, such as the American Battle Monuments Commission sites in France. Serbs, having lost some 28% of their total population in the war, erected the famed Monument to the Unknown Hero close to the capital, Belgrade.

Even though the war had ended, much work remained to ensure lasting stability. In an effort to prevent another major global conflict, world leaders established the League of Nations in 1920 as part of the Treaty of Versailles. This international organization was dedicated to maintaining peace and resolving disputes through diplomacy. Although the League had notable successes in mediating conflicts during the 1920s, it ultimately lacked the authority and enforcement mechanisms necessary to prevent future aggression, as the world came to realize in the late 1930s. One of the League's major flaws was the absence of key world powers. The United States, despite President Woodrow Wilson's advocacy for the League, never joined due to opposition in the U.S. Senate. Germany and the Soviet Union were initially excluded, and Japan and Italy would later withdraw as they pursued expansionist policies. The League's weaknesses would become apparent

WORLD WAR 1

as the world once again teetered on the precipice of an all-encompassing and savage war.

1914 portrait photograph of Woodrow Wilson.

WORLD WAR 1

As such, we can see that the Great War's end did not deliver peace and stability on a silver platter. Instead, it brought an end to death and destruction, and a beginning of many new challenges. But despite their hardships, people came together to revive their economies, rebuild their cities, calm their societies' political and social upheavals, and ultimately, mourn their dead.

Chapter 10:
Freedom's Bitter Taste

One would think that the war's end would bring about a much-needed breath of fresh air, free from the smell of gunpowder, from the constant rain of artillery shells, and the massive loss of life. But it was not to be. The war shook the world and had significant repercussions across the globe. And so it was that the post-war years brought further conflicts to some nations. Ireland was one of them. Its constant, growing desire to be independent and free from British rule caused great tumult in the country, ultimately leading to the 1916 Easter Rebellion (*Éirí Amach na Cásca*). Lasting from April 24th to 29th, 1916, it ended in complete failure for the Irish Republicans. However, even though the uprising failed, it led to a further distancing between Ireland and Britain. And when the British were forced to attempt military conscription in Ireland in 1918, a new crisis emerged. Ultimately, it was the deep social unrest from these incidents that led to the Irish War of Independence (*Cogadh na Saoirse*), which lasted from 1919 to 1921. It was one of the major conflicts that occurred in the aftermath of the First World War, and it ended in a ceasefire. The Anglo-Irish treaty followed and resulted in the partition of Ireland. It was through this partition that the Irish Free State was created, a state independent from the United Kingdom, but still a part of the British Empire, and with a portion that remained under direct British Rule: Northern Ireland. So, we can see that the world map became considerably different after the First World War. Numerous countries gained their independence for the very first time, and this made for a distinct socio-political and ethno-cultural map, one that would be a crucial setting for the Second World War, which was — unbeknownst to the world — not too far in the future.

WORLD WAR 1

Dublin in the aftermath of the 1916 Rising.

In the faraway Caucasus mountains, the nation of Armenia gained independence from the Russian Empire for the first time since the Middle Ages, as did its close neighbor, Georgia. Estonia and Finland also got rid of the shackles of the Russian Empire, snatching their long-sought independence, as did neighboring Latvia and Lithuania. And with the collapse of Austria-Hungary, many neighboring and newly emerged states staked their territorial claims: Italy took from the ruins of the Empire Trieste, South Tyrol, and Istria; Czechoslovakia claimed Moravia, parts of Silesia, and Bohemia; Romania took control over the Hungarian parts of Banat, Maramures, and the

Austrian regions of Bukovina; while the Kingdom of Serbs, Croats, and Slovenes that was Yugoslavia took from Austria the Kingdom of Dalmatia and the Duchy of Carniola, and from Hungary the parts of Banat, Bacska, and Baranya..

Another major and quite significant event that occurred following the Great War left deep and irreversible scars on the entire world. Known as the Spanish Flu, the 1918 influenza epidemic was one of the most fatal virus outbreaks in human history and claimed 50 to 100 million lives. It lasted from 1918, while the Great War still raged, and until April 1920. During its run, the Spanish Flu infected close to 500 million people, which at the time was one-third of the global population. The Spanish Flu was first documented in the United States when, on March 4th, 1918, army cook Gitchell Albert was diagnosed at Camp Funston in Kansas. There were further cases diagnosed in Fort Riley in Kansas, and even more in New York City. With the entry of the United States Army into the European Theatre of the Great War, the virus spread rapidly, reaching France, Britain, and Germany. The origin of the name "Spanish flu" is unknown. Spain at the time was a neutral country. But there were contemporary sources that mentioned the illness of the Spanish King, Alfonso, which would account for the origin of the term "Spanish" flu. However, the name was not universal and was known by other names in different regions: "Bolshevik Disease" in Poland or "German Flu" in Brazil. But no matter its name, one factor remained constant: it spread like wildfire. By May 1918, it had reached Poland, Japan, North Africa, India, and even China and Australia. The first six months of the flu's deadly reign were not too severe, as deaths were moderate and did not cause widespread alarm. But the second wave that arrived in 1918 was truly horrifying and took the world by surprise. Troop movements around the world caused the disease to spread with unprecedented speed, reaching virtually every corner of the globe. And it was this second wave that proved to be most fatal. In just three months, there were close to 300,000 deaths in the United States alone. In India, roughly 20 million lives were lost in 1918, while in Europe, major capital cities numbered their dead in the tens of thousands. A third wave of the virus attacked Europe in 1919, claiming further hundreds of thousands of lives across many nations, and was followed by the fourth and final wave in 1920.

For the entire world, the loss of life was an enormous catastrophe. The millions of casualties of the Great War were a tragedy in and of themselves, but were made even worse by the additional millions of Spanish Flu victims. In the

United States, where the flu is thought to have originated, almost 850,000 people lost their lives. Particularly affected were the Native American communities, as they lived in small settlements and were much more vulnerable to epidemics. Entire villages were wiped out as a result. To the south, in Brazil, the death toll reached 300,000. In Europe, France lost close to 400,000 citizens, while in Britain this number was smaller: 250,000. Japan was also hit very hard by the virus: 23 million people were infected, with more than 390,000 dying as a result. The Russians were hit hard as well, with a reported 450,000 deaths.

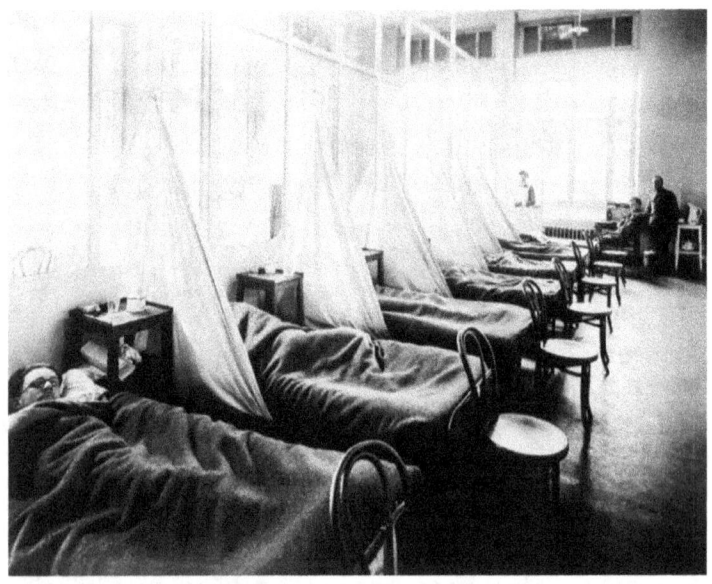

Flu patients, France, 1918.

WORLD WAR 1

The Spanish Flu disrupted normal life throughout the world. Entire communities and nations were impacted, particularly in less-developed areas and in places where there were pronounced age differences. Some towns were practically depopulated, with most of their adults succumbing to the disease. Healthcare was heavily affected, as was the economy. In several reported cases, the death toll was so devastatingly high that the dead could not be buried. This resulted in many mass graves, in which the dead were laid without coffins. Alaska is a clear example of just how devastating such an outbreak can be. Its remote Inuit communities were heavily impacted: many of their villages ceased to exist. Forty percent of Alaska's Inuit population died of influenza.

Remote communities in the Pacific also suffered immensely, as the indigenous tribes, many still living their ancient, traditional lifestyles, were unable to effectively combat the invisible threat. The small Pacific nation of Nauru lost a devastating 16% of its entire population, while Tonga lost 8%. One of the worst cases of loss of life was in Western Samoa. When the flu reached these remote islands, it spread like a black, deathly cloud and infected 90% of the population there. The ultimate death toll was crushing: 30% of the men died, 22% of the women, and 10% of the children.

Elsewhere in the world, regions that previously suffered from mass starvation and poverty were hit particularly hard. Iran, for example, was dealing with the effects of the Persian Famine of 1917 to 1919, when it was struck by the deadly disease. As the two calamities combined, death reigned freely, claiming 2,430,000 lives. It is these incredible stories of catastrophe and what people had to endure that give us a crucial insight into the state of the world in the years after the Great War. Its far-reaching shadow did not fall merely on the battlefields and blood-drenched trenches. It extended beyond the war, resulting in poverty, hunger, and ultimately, disease — burdens that, in many cases, sometimes proved more devastating than the war itself.

Just like the ripples on the surface of a pond, the war's repercussions spread across the globe and changed the fate of humankind forever. They brought radical political, economic, and cultural changes that ushered the world into an entirely new era.

Additionally, the Spanish Flu of 1918 offers us vital lessons for our modern age, particularly compared to diseases appearing in our own time, such as the recent COVID-19 pandemic. Both the Spanish Flu epidemic and the COVID-19 pandemic reveal how quickly infectious diseases can spread in a highly connected world and the importance of early, transparent communication from governments and health authorities. During the Spanish Flu, delayed responses and inconsistent public health messaging contributed to higher death tolls, a pattern that echoed in the early stages of COVID-19. Also, both crises highlighted the significance of non-pharmaceutical interventions. Measures such as social distancing, wearing protective face masks, and major public hygiene campaigns were critical in mitigating transmission before vaccines became widely available. By examining the missteps and successes of the past, modern societies can better understand the value of preparedness, trust in science, and global cooperation in managing future public health emergencies.

The Great War undoubtedly has an infamous reputation as one of the deadliest conflicts in the collective human history — a reputation that endures to this day. Involving all major European powers and spreading across the globe, the war led to the mobilization of millions of men. But it was not only the soldiers who became the victims of this terrible war: civilians did as well. When we examine the official death statistics, we find that they tend to vary and are obtained from a variety of sources (much like statistics from today's conflicts).

The statistics reported by each country involved in the war can be somewhat biased, particularly those released in the war's immediate aftermath. Even so, the sheer devastation and the scale of the Great War are undeniable. It was a whirlwind of hatred that claimed countless lives, both young and old. All unbiased sources generally agree that the grand total of both civilian and military casualties in the First World War is around 40 million. Of those, deaths account for between 15 to 22 million, with approximately 23 million wounded.

A fact that truly provides us with a proper perspective and gives us key insights into just how devastating the war was for civilian populations is the difference between military and civilian deaths. Military deaths amounted to between 9 and 11 million, while civilian deaths ranged from 6 to 13 million. Digging deeper into the numbers, we see that the Central Powers lost roughly 4 million men, while the Allies lost about 6 million. Furthermore, the sources all agree that roughly 2 million people lost their lives due to a variety of diseases that ran rampant during the war, while close to 6 million were proclaimed missing and presumed dead. With the Great War likely being the first truly modern conflict, we can also observe a significant change in the causes of death from past wars, due to the noticeable shift in methods of warfare. Prior to the war, disease had been the chief contributor to war deaths toll. With the advancements in warfare during the First World War, the primary cause of death shifted to battlefield casualties.

Being that the Great War affected many countries, from Asia to Europe to Africa, some nations also suffered greatly from the disproportionate ratio between their overall population and military personnel numbers. A good example is Serbia, the nation that suffered the wrath of Austria-Hungary and bore the Great War's first blows. The Kingdom of Serbia was smaller than it is today, and the rapid rise of casualties in the early stages of the war had a major impact on its populace. Military deaths were immense: the Serbian Army rapidly diminished from 420,000 to just 100,000 men. The subsequent arrival of the Spanish Flu and a typhus epidemic took a further toll, and the Serbian nation ultimately lost a significant percentage of its entire population. It is generally agreed that the Serbian casualties constituted 8% of all Allied wartime losses. When put into perspective, this was an enormous and devastating loss for this small and struggling Balkan nation. Furthermore, Serbia lost around 29% of its entire population, and perhaps

60% of its male population. After the war, 500,000 children were left as orphans. Serbia is just one example of several nations that suffered such incomprehensible losses during the war, losses that would permanently reflect their futures.

The tremendous loss of life cannot be attributed only to war's cruel mechanisms. As we covered earlier, the 50 to 100 million claimed by the Spanish Flu added to the toll, deepening the tragic story of loss and shifting the course of our shared history in an ever darker direction.

Tragically, massacres and genocides were significant contributors to the war's staggering death toll. Conflict, war, and strife bring humanity's darkest traits to the surface. In this sense, the Great War was a grim turning point that marked the end of old notions of chivalry and the slower, more structured warfare of the musket and cavalry era. This was a war of bitterness and far-reaching conflicts, a war in which the accumulated resentments of entire peoples and generations quickly erupted to reveal the ugly side of every man and woman. Numerous major powers descended into the crime of ethnic cleansing as the war progressed and took on a more chaotic side.

An infamous example of this is the ethnic cleansing of the Armenian population by the Ottoman

Empire. In its final years, the Ottoman Empire organized and carried out mass executions of its Armenian populace, a direct result of ethnic tensions that had simmered for generations. The Ottomans organized this mass expulsion between 1914 and 1923, which resulted in approximately 1.5 million Armenian deaths — one of the worst tragedies in the history of the Armenian people. A similar genocide, also instigated by the Ottomans, occurred in Greece in the same period and resulted in close to 750,000 Greek deaths.

As the Great War descended on an unsuspecting world, the nationalistic tensions that had run rampant in the years preceding it finally broke forth. The war caused major strife between certain ethnicities, and long-lost simmering tensions that had lain dormant up to that point were rekindled and brought to a sudden boil. As soon as the war began, Austro-Hungarian soldiers carried out numerous massacres in Serbia, focusing their wrath on the nation's peaceful, agrarian population. There were many factors that contributed to such wanton hate. At the time, Austria-Hungary was a multi-ethnic nation. Among the ranks of its military were many Croats, Slovenes, Muslims, and Hungarians, all of whom harbored great ethnic hatred toward the Serbs. The first stages of the war saw them massacring Serb villagers, mostly along the invasion route in western Serbia. Eastern Serbia, on the other hand, saw the evil of the Bulgarian soldiers, whose centuries of hatred toward the Serbs erupted. One infamous event was the Surdulica massacre, where the Bulgarians killed roughly 3,000 Serbs.

The remains of Serbs massacred by Bulgarian soldiers in the town of Surdulica.

To make matters even worse, some Serbs were ordered to fight against…Serbs. Those Serbs who had lived for centuries in Croatia (another Austro-Hungarian territory) were also conscripted into the Austro-Hungarian army and ordered to fight against their own kin. This caused many Serb soldiers to desert, and they fled either to their Serbian brothers on the other side or to the Russian forces, as they did not want to kill their own kin.

Another such grim episode is the so-called Rape of Belgium, which occurred in the war's early stages, when Germany invaded this small and neutral Western European nation. Notoriously, the Germans were harsh in dealing with incidents of sabotage and opposition from the conquered nation (much the same as what would happen in the Second World War). After the invasion of Belgium, the Germans retaliated against the sabotaging of rail lines and similar acts of defiance by mass-shooting suspects and saboteurs. They also suspected that all civilians were possible guerrilla fighters, and this resulted in them massacring more than 6,500 Belgian and French civilians between August and November 1914. The Germans also resorted to destroying numerous important and historic buildings as a form of punishment for sabotage. Of these, the most notable was a historic university library in the city of Louvain.

War never changes. Whatever form it takes, it is essentially the same: a cruel and chaotic display of human nature in its worst aspects. And wherever

WORLD WAR 1

war comes, death soon follows. But when the Great War began, the scale suddenly grew incredibly larger. Industry came, and with it the cruel weapons of mass destruction, instruments of pain that reaped lives across Europe. As old and new were entwined in a grim dance, death emerged crowned.

Conclusion

The First World War — hailed at the time as "The War to End All Wars" — failed to deliver the lasting peace its contemporaries hoped for. Instead, it reshaped the 20th century and the modern world with an intensity few could have foreseen. The war shattered empires, redrew borders, and unleashed social and political upheavals whose reverberations are still felt today. From the collapse of the Habsburg, Ottoman, Russian, and German empires, to the rise of new ideologies like communism and fascism, the conflict left in its wake a transformed global order and a deeply scarred generation.

The unprecedented scale of industrialized slaughter on the Western Front, defined by trenches, mud, barbed wire, and unrelenting artillery fire, fundamentally changed the way nations perceived war. No longer could it be seen as a romantic, noble, or glorious pursuit. Instead, it exposed the terrifying power of modern technology in the service of destruction. Millions of lives were lost not only on the battlefield but also in the pandemics, famines, and displacements that followed. And yet, amid the horror, humanity revealed its resilience: soldiers helped one another survive impossible odds; artists, writers, and poets captured the human condition with raw, haunting brilliance; and from the ashes of destruction, societies began to rebuild.

The Treaty of Versailles, intended as a means of closure, instead sowed seeds of resentment and economic instability that would eventually ignite another, even more devastating, world conflict. Thus, World War I must be remembered not only for what it destroyed, but also for what it foretold. It marked the end of an old world and the reluctant birth of a new one — one where nationalism, modern warfare, and mass politics would redefine every corner of the globe.

More than a century later, we look back not only to mourn the dead or to study the movements of armies, but to understand the profound human choices and fragile consequences of power. The Great War stands as a monument to both human failure, resilience, and perseverance. In remembering it, we honor those who suffered and commit ourselves to preventing such a calamity — one born of ambition, misunderstanding, and callous disregard for life — from ever recurring.

WORLD WAR 1

History does not end; it flows forward, shaped by memory and meaning. Thus, the story of the Great War lives on, not only in books and memorials, but in the enduring hope that through understanding, we may yet learn to choose peace.

References:

Books & Academic References

Babac, D. (2016). *The Serbian Army in the Great War 1914–1918*. Helion & Company.

Beckett, F. W. I. (2014). *The Great War: 1914–1918*. Routledge.

Bridger, G. (2009). *The Great War Handbook*. Pen & Sword.

Dowling, C. T. (2014). Eastern Front. In *International Encyclopedia of the First World War*. https://encyclopedia.1914-1918-online.net/article/eastern_front

Fussell, P. (2000). *The Great War and Modern Memory*. Oxford University Press.

Hart, P. (2013). *The Great War: A Combat History of the First World War*. Oxford University Press.

Mitrović, A. (2007). *Serbia's Great War, 1914–1918*. Purdue University Press.

Winter, J. (Ed.). (2014). *The Cambridge History of the First World War: Volume I – Global War*. Cambridge University Press.

Winter, J. (Ed.). (2014). *The Cambridge History of the First World War: Volume II – The State*. Cambridge University Press.

Winter, J. (Ed.). (2014). *The Cambridge History of the First World War: Volume III – Civil Society*. Cambridge University Press.

Willmott, H. P. (2003). *First World War*. Dorling Kindersley.

Primary Sources – Letters, Speeches & Diaries

Churchill, W. (1917). *Speech as Minister of Munitions on women's employment during the Great War*. United Kingdom government publication. Presumed public domain.

Fearns, B. (1917). *Recollection of the Battle of Poelcappelle*. Personal diary entry or oral history. Source unverified; used under fair use for educational purposes.

Gilson, R. (1915, May 12). *Letter to his mother from the Western Front*. Personal correspondence. Presumed public domain.

Stewart, E. H. C. (1916, ca. June). *Letter from the Western Front*. Personal correspondence. Presumed public domain.

WORLD WAR 1

Symons, J. G. (1915, ca. late year). *Letter from France during WWI*. Personal correspondence. Presumed public domain.

Anonymous. (1917). *Letter from a field hospital in France*. Personal correspondence. Presumed public domain.

Image References

Archduke Franz Ferdinand minutes before the assassination. (1914). Source: Wikimedia Commons. Retrieved from https://upload.wikimedia.org/wikipedia/commons/b/b7/Postcard_for_the_assassination_of_Archduke_Franz_Ferdinand_in_Sarajevo.jpg

German soldiers on the way to the Front. (1914). Source: Wikimedia Commons. Retrieved from https://upload.wikimedia.org/wikipedia/commons/c/c0/German_soldiers_in_a_railroad_car_on_the_way_to_the_front_during_early_World_War_I%2C_taken_in_1914._Taken_from_greatwar.nl_site.jpg

Serbian airplane. (1915). Source: Wikimedia Commons. Retrieved from https://upload.wikimedia.org/wikipedia/commons/a/a6/FirstSerbianArmedPlane1915.jpg

Ruins of Carency, Western Front. (1915). Source: Wikimedia Commons. Retrieved from https://upload.wikimedia.org/wikipedia/commons/5/5e/Capture_of_Carency_aftermath_1915_1.jpg

Australian infantry wearing Small Box Respirators (SBR), 45th Battalion. (1917). Source: Wikimedia Commons. Retrieved from https://upload.wikimedia.org/wikipedia/commons/3/34/Australian_infantry_small_box_respirators_Ypres_1917.jpg

The Munitions Girls, Stanhope Forbes. (1918). Source: Wikimedia Commons. Retrieved from https://upload.wikimedia.org/wikipedia/commons/7/76/%27The_Munitions_Girls%27_oil_painting%2C_England%2C_1918_Wellcome_L0059548.jpg

American nurses at a Red Cross hospital, Liverpool. (n.d.). Source: Wikimedia Commons. Retrieved from https://upload.wikimedia.org/wikipedia/commons/0/0f/The_Red_Cross_during_the_First_World_War_Q44160.jpg

Big Tank Lumbering into Action over a Trench. (1919). Source: Wikimedia Commons. Retrieved from https://upload.wikimedia.org/wikipedia/commons/6/6f/The_people%27s_war_book%3B_history%2C_cyclopaedia_and_chronology_of_the_grea

WORLD WAR 1

t_world_war_%281919%29_%2814595055920%29.jpg

Type of gas mask used by the English to protect men and horses. (1915). Source: Wikimedia Commons. Retrieved from https://upload.wikimedia.org/wikipedia/commons/f/f2/The_Great_war_%281915%29_%2814578365160%29.jpg

BE 2c 90hp RAF 1A engine in flight. (n.d.). Source: Wikimedia Commons. Retrieved from https://upload.wikimedia.org/wikipedia/commons/4/42/Aircraft_of_the_First_World_War_Q33852.jpg

Emergency Hospital during the Spanish Flu epidemic. (1918). Source: Wikimedia Commons. Retrieved from https://upload.wikimedia.org/wikipedia/commons/2/20/Emergency_hospital_during_Influenza_epidemic%2C_Camp_Funston%2C_Kansas_-_NCP_1603.jpg

Russian troops going to the frontline. (n.d.). Source: Wikimedia Commons. Retrieved from https://upload.wikimedia.org/wikipedia/commons/7/72/Russian_Troops_NGM-v31-p372.jpg

German auxiliary cruiser SMS Seeadler. (n.d.). Source: Wikimedia Commons. Retrieved from https://upload.wikimedia.org/wikipedia/commons/2/2c/SMSSeeadlerFront.PNG

German trenches in German Cameroon. (n.d.). Source: Wikimedia Commons. Retrieved from https://upload.wikimedia.org/wikipedia/commons/a/a0/German_trenches_in_Garua.jpg

Paul von Lettow-Vorbeck, Lion of Africa. (n.d.). Source: Wikimedia Commons. Retrieved from https://upload.wikimedia.org/wikipedia/commons/b/b7/General_Paul_von_Lettow-Vorbeck_LCCN2014719610b.jpg

Cartoon – France vs. Germany over Alsace-Lorraine. (1898). Source: Wikimedia Commons. Retrieved from https://upload.wikimedia.org/wikipedia/commons/c/c2/A_new_legend_in_an_old_dress_-_Keppler._LCCN2012647516.jpg

British propaganda poster – Kitchener wants you. (1914). Source: Wikimedia Commons. Retrieved from https://upload.wikimedia.org/wikipedia/commons/0/01/30a_Sammlung_Eybl_Gro%C3%9Fbritannien._Alfred_Leete_%281882%E2%80%931933%29_Britons_%28Kitchener%29_wants_you_%28Briten_Kitchener_braucht_Euch%29._1914_%28Nachdruck%29%2C_74_x_50_cm._%28Slg.Nr._552%29.jpg

WORLD WAR 1

German soldiers in a trench. (1916). Source: Wikimedia Commons. Retrieved from https://upload.wikimedia.org/wikipedia/commons/6/6c/Bundesarchiv_Bild_136-B0560%2C_Frankreich%2C_Kavalleristen_im_Sch%C3%BCtzengraben.jpg

Trenches of the 11th Cheshire Regiment, Somme. (1916). Source: Wikimedia Commons. Retrieved from https://upload.wikimedia.org/wikipedia/commons/f/fa/Cheshire_Regiment_trench_Somme_1916.jpg

Destroyed German trench on the Western Front. (n.d.). Source: Wikimedia Commons. Retrieved from https://upload.wikimedia.org/wikipedia/commons/4/47/NLS_Haig_-_Smashed_up_German_trench_on_Messines_Ridge_with_dead.jpg

The wagon in which the armistice was signed. (1918). Source: Wikimedia Commons. Retrieved from https://upload.wikimedia.org/wikipedia/commons/2/21/Armisticetrain.jpg

Ruins of Ypres. (1919). Source: Wikimedia Commons. Retrieved from https://upload.wikimedia.org/wikipedia/commo

WORLD WAR 1

ns/2/2f/Ru%C3%AFne%2C_1919%2C_Ieper.jpg

Portrait photograph of Woodrow Wilson. (1914). Source: Wikimedia Commons. Retrieved from https://upload.wikimedia.org/wikipedia/commons/b/b4/President_Woodrow_Wilson_in_1914%2C_Harris_%26_Ewing_%283x4_cropped_b%29.jpg

Dublin after the 1916 Rising. (1916). Source: Wikimedia Commons. Retrieved from https://upload.wikimedia.org/wikipedia/commons/5/5b/The_shell_of_the_G.P.O._on_Sackville_Street_after_the_Easter_Rising_%286937669789%29.jpg

Flu patients, France. (1918). Source: Wikimedia Commons. Retrieved from https://upload.wikimedia.org/wikipedia/commons/9/98/USCampHospital45InfluenzaWard.jpg

Remains of Serbs massacred by Bulgarian soldiers, Surdulica. (n.d.). Source: Wikimedia Commons. Retrieved from https://upload.wikimedia.org/wikipedia/commons/0/06/Ostatky_Srb%C5%AF_povra%C5%BEd%C4%9Bn%C3%BDch_Bulhary.jpg

FREE BONUS FROM HBA: EBOOK BUNDLE

Greetings!

First, thank you for reading our books.

Now, we invite you to join our VIP list. As a welcome gift, we offer the History & Mythology eBook Bundle below for free. Plus, you can be the first to receive new books and exclusives! Remember, it's 100% free to join.

Simply click the link below to join.

https://www.subscribepage.com/hba

Keep up to date with us on:
YouTube: History Brought Alive
Facebook: History Brought Alive
www.historybroughtalive.com

OTHER BOOKS BY HISTORY BROUGHT ALIVE

Available on all major retailers

- History of India: A Concise Introduction to Indian History, Culture, Mythology, Religion, Gandhi, Characters, Empires, Achievements & More Throughout The Ages

- Native American Wisdom: A Comprehensive Guide to The History, Culture & Herbal Healing Practices of Indigenous Americans (2 Books in 1)

- Scotland: A Journey through Scottish History, Battles, Clans, Highlanders, Myths, Legends & More

- Roman Legends For Kids: Emperors, Gladiators, Heroes, Myths & More from Ancient Rome

- Norse Mythology Legends: Epic Stories, Quests, Myths & More from The Most Powerful Characters, Gods, Goddesses & Heroes of Norse & Viking Folklore

WORLD WAR 1

- Norse Paganism for Beginners: Explore The History of The Old Norse Religion - Asatru, Cosmology, Astrology, Mythology, Magic, Runes, Tarot, Witchcraft & More

- Reckoning of Power: Oppenheimer, the Atomic Bomb & World War 2

- Roman Empire: Rise & The Fall. Explore The History, Mythology, Legends, Epic Battles & Lives Of The Emperors, Legions, Heroes, Gladiators & More

- The Vikings: Who Were The Vikings? Enter The Viking Age & Discover The Facts, Sagas, Norse Mythology, Legends, Battles & More

- The History of China: A Concise Introduction to Chinese History, Culture, Dynasties, Mythology, Great Achievements & More of The Oldest Living Civilization

- The History of England: An Introduction to Centuries of English Culture, Kings & Queens, Key Events, Battles & More

- The Vikings: Who Were The Vikings? Enter The Viking Age & Discover The Facts, Sagas, Norse Mythology, Legends, Battles & More

WORLD WAR 1

- Native American History: Accurate & Comprehensive History, Origins, Culture, Tribes, Legends, Mythology, Wars, Stories & More of The Native Indigenous Americans

- Norse Magic & Runes: A Guide To The Magic, Rituals, Spells & Meanings of Norse Magick, Mythology & Reading The Elder Futhark Runes

- Norse Mythology: Captivating Stories & Timeless Tales Of Norse Folklore. The Myths, Sagas & Legends of The Gods, Immortals, Magical Creatures, Vikings & More

- Norse Mythology, Magic & Romance: A Trilogy of History, Mythology, Paganism & Viking Folklore + A Fictional Nordic Tale: 3 books (3 books in 1)

- Norse Mythology, Vikings, Magic & Runes: Stories, Legends & Timeless Tales From Norse & Viking Folklore + A Guide To The Rituals, Spells & Meanings of ... Elder Futhark Runes: 3 books (3 books in 1)

- Japanese History: Explore The Magnificent History, Culture, Mythology, Folklore, Wars,

WORLD WAR 1

Legends, Great Achievements & More Of Japan

- Mesoamerican History & Mythology

- Mythology of Mesopotamia: Fascinating Insights, Myths, Stories & History From The World's Most Ancient Civilization. Sumerian, Akkadian, Babylonian, Persian, Assyrian, and More

- Native American Herbalism: Improve Your Health, Wellness & Vitality with Indigenous Healing Practices, Medicinal Plants, Natural Herbs, & Herbalist Remedies

- History of Asia: Explore The Magnificent Histories, Culture, Mythology, Folklore, Wars, Legends, Stories, Achievements & More of China, Japan & India(3 Books in 1)

- Hoodoo for Beginners: Connect To The Ancient Spirit World of Africa & Manifest Success With Spells, Root Magic, Conjuring, Herbs, Traditions, History & More

- Irish History & Mythology: Exploring The History, Celtic Myths, Folklore, Sagas, Traditions of Ireland (British Isles Book 3)

WORLD WAR 1

- EL IMPERIO ROMANO: Auge Y Caída De Roma. Explora La Historia, La Mitología, Las Leyendas, Las Batallas Épicas Y Las Vidas De Los Emperadores, Las Legiones, ... Los Gladiadores Y Más (Spanish Edition)

- Greek Mythology: Explore The Timeless Tales Of Ancient Greece, The Myths, History & Legends of The Gods, Goddesses, Titans, Heroes, Monsters & More

- Greek, Mesopotamia, Egypt & Rome: Fascinating Insights, Mythology, Stories, History & Knowledge From The World's Most Interesting Civilizations & Empires: 4 books

- African History: Explore The Amazing Timeline of The World's Richest Continent - The History, Culture, Folklore, Mythology & More of Africa

- African History & Hoodoo: Connect to The Ancient Spirit of Africa and Explore The Timeline, Culture, Roots, Spells, & More From The World's Richest Continent (2 Books in 1)

- Ancient Egypt: Discover Fascinating History, Mythology, Gods, Goddesses, Pharaohs,

WORLD WAR 1

Pyramids & More From The Mysterious Ancient Egyptian Civilisation

- Celtic Mythology & History: Explore Timeless Tales, Folklore, Religion, Magic, Legendary Stories & More: Ireland, Scotland, Great Britain, Wales

For Kids

- African Legends For Kids: Kings, Queens, Heroes, Spirits, Myths, Tales & More From Africa

- Aztec Legends For Kids: Gods, Warriors, Myths, Wonders & More From Ancient Mexico

- Celtic Legends For Kids: Heroes, Fairies, Warriors, Myths, Magic & More From The Ancient Celts

- Chinese Legends For Kids: Emperors, Dragons, Gods, Heroes, Myths & More From Ancient China

- English Legends For Kids: Knights, Castles, Kings, Queens, Myths & More From Old England

WORLD WAR 1

- Incan Legends For Kids: Emperors, Warriors, Myths, Treasures & More From Ancient Peru

- Indian Legends For Kids: Gods, Goddesses, Warriors, Sages, Myths, Epics & More From Ancient India

- Irish Legends For Kids: Heroes, Druids, Myths, Magic & More From Ancient Ireland

- Japanese Legends For Kids: Samurai, Spirits, Emperors, Myths, Magic & More From Japan

- Mesopotamian Legends For Kids: Kings, Queens, Gods, Myths, Wonders & More From The Cradle Of Civilization

- Native American Legends For Kids: Spirits, Chiefs, Warriors, Myths, Sacred Tales & More

- Persian Legends For Kids: Heroes, Kings, Myths, Epics & More From Ancient Persia

- Russian Legends For Kids: Czars, Fairies, Warriors, Folktales, Myths & More From Russia

- Scottish Legends For Kids: Warriors, Fairies, Kings, Queens, Myths, Legends & More From Scotland

WORLD WAR 1

- Thai Legends For Kids: Kings, Queens, Demons, Heroes, Myths, Sacred Tales & More From Thailand

- Viking & Norse Legends For Kids: Gods, Warriors, Myths, Heroes & More From The Ancient Norse World

- Welsh Legends For Kids: Dragons, Heroes, Prophecies, Myths, Magic & More From Ancient Wales

and follow us on www.historybroughtalive.com and https://www.youtube.com/@historybroughtalive

www.ingramcontent.com/pod-product-compliance
Lightning Source LLC
Chambersburg PA
CBHW050341010526
44119CB00049B/642